Walking in Grace

ONE WOMAN'S STORY OF HEALING BY THE POWER OF GOD

PAMELA PORTER

Praise for Walking in Grace

Psalm 34:4 (NIV) “I sought the Lord, and he answered me; He delivered me from all my fears.” The passage above could be used to summarize the experiences described in Walking In Grace. The author in this non-fiction narrative, in a very eloquent voice, describes how she met and overcame an unexpected challenge. While not prescriptive, this descriptive account provides personal witness to the strength of ancestral and spiritual roots. In her very efficient writing style, the author invites the reader to join her as she traverses the rough territory from uncertainty to victory. This book is written for readers of all age groups, young adults, and mature readers.

- **Review by Walter Morris Baker, PhD.**

The talent of this writer is amazing! Reading this book is as stimulating as an episode of “Watson”, featuring a physician who treats patients with mysterious medical conditions. Mrs. Porter shares not one but two medical mysteries. This along with the parallel family storyline emphasizes the sovereignty of God’s timing.

Her transparency and attention to details bring the reader alongside her, in the hospital room. I am grateful that Mrs. Porter shared her journey to educate others about a condition that has been silenced by its invisible pain and suffering.

We can clearly see a mindset shift by this author which creates the medium necessary to masterfully usher us to the climax of her experience.

Spiritually, the ending is powerful. Mrs. Porter's values including faith, family and prayer were driving forces to carry her when everything else seems to fail.

I could not put the book down and was able to finish it in two sessions. This book touches every emotion humanly possible. Get ready for a heart-wrenching but mind-blowing read!

- Kathy C. Scott-Gurnell, MD

This is a beautifully written, personal story about hardship and faith.

- Sherry Fleming Ed.D, Psychologist

Riveting, Powerful and Encouraging describes this life-changing faith story from author, Pamela Porter. Prepare to cry, laugh & rejoice through this faith-enduring journey that every child, spouse and/or parent will identify with. Her testimony of encountering the love and healing of God in her worst hour will fill your heart with hope to believe in the Goodness of God... *just wow*!

Todd Knight
Sr. Pastoral Leadership Team, Antioch Ft. Worth

Walking in Grace

This book is a work of memoir. It is based on the author's personal experiences, reflections, and recollections. While the events described are true to the best of the author's memory, some names, identifying details, and circumstances have been changed to protect the privacy of individuals. Any resemblance to actual persons, living or dead, beyond what is intentional, is coincidental.

This book is not intended as medical, psychological, or professional advice. The author is not a medical professional, and any medical information or experiences described are shared solely from a personal perspective. Readers are encouraged to seek appropriate professional counsel regarding their own health or circumstances.

ISBN: 978-1-943563-15-9

Published by ML Stimpson Enterprises

P.O. Box 1592

Cedar Hill, TX 75104-1592

Printed in the United States of America

Contents

Dedication

This book is lovingly dedicated to Grandmother Sadie for setting me on a path of walking and talking with Jesus.

To our wonderful children, Lauren, Quentin, Ryan, and Caitlin. I've always needed you more than you needed me.

To our precious grandchildren, Cameron, Landon, and Noa. You are light in my world and joy in my heart.

And above all, to my dear husband, Ralph. Words fail me in expressing my level of gratitude, love, and respect for you. My soul appreciates the way I feel about you. God knew exactly who I needed as my life partner and my anchor. Your dedication and support have held me up when I literally could not stand. Your strength is my strength. Your love is my life force and motivation in my hardest moments.

You were my then. You are my now. You are my forever.

I love you, babe.

Acknowledgments

This book would not exist without the love, support, and encouragement of so many people who walked beside me on my journey—far too many to list but know that you are appreciated.

First, I thank my husband, Ralph, for his patience and unwavering support throughout, not only this writing process, but the trials that led up to this moment. Your love carried me through when I literally could not even stand. Thank you for believing in me, especially when I was tired or questioning my abilities. You are my person. I love you, babe.

To my family members who were subjected to my constant "my book" comments, thank you for listening, praying, and cheering me on. You lift my spirits on the hard days and bring such joy in my life.

To my dear friends, church family and former colleagues, thank you for covering me in prayer and reminding me of my purpose. Thanks also, for the laughs exactly when I needed them.

A heartfelt thank-you to Chrystal Evans Hurst for your

willingness to open that first door that has led to getting my book into reader's hands. I am forever grateful to you.

I am especially grateful to my editor, Rhonda McKnight, for her passion for this passion. You saw the power in my testimony and the potential for its impact. Your meticulous attention to detail taught this novice author more than I could imagine.

To my publisher, Michelle Stimpson, thank you for jumping right in, believing in my story, and keeping me on track, all the way to the finish line. Your encouragement and steady direction were exactly what I needed.

Above all, I give thanks to my Heavenly Father. Your love, faithfulness, and strength brought me through. You gave me this testimony and equipped me to share Your message of hope and healing to all who read it. All the glory and honor is Yours.

Introduction

I've considered myself a writer since I first picked up a crayon and scribbled what I was *convinced* were words. My bedroom, school backpack, and the back seat of our car were my personal libraries. Surrounded by books was my happy place. The written word is my passion and my escape from life's realities. So, I align myself with fellow writers when I say we must never let the opinion of others keep us from sharing our truth and our God-given gift for storytelling.

That's not to say that I didn't wrestle with keeping the secret to myself since the morning my life was transformed. I certainly did. But God gave me this testimony, not to keep hidden, but to share as a message of hope for others.

My first hurdle was to get out of God's way and let Him use me. Initially, imposter syndrome stole my confidence because I let it gain an unearned foothold. Anxiety caused me to question my writing ability and the believability of my testimony.

During anxious prayers, God met me in *Exodus 4:10-12* before I faced my blank laptop screen.

"But Moses pleaded with the Lord, "O Lord, I'm not very good with words. I never have been, and I'm not now, even though

you have spoken to me. I get tongue-tied, and my words get tangled."

Then the Lord asked Moses, "Who makes a person's mouth? Who decides whether people speak or do not speak, hear or do not hear, see or do not see? Is it not I, the Lord? Now go! I will be with you as you speak, and I will instruct you in what to say."

Just as God assured Moses that He would equip him with the words and ability to be an orator and leader, He met me at the keyboard with that same gift of confidence. God's voice played repeatedly in my mind: "Tell Them." If I trusted Him for my life-changing moment in April 2018, I could certainly trust Him to share it now.

A disclaimer is necessary at this point. I am not a medical professional. Medical information shared in this story is my best interpretation in layman's terms. The focus of this book is my transformative experience rather than medical jargon.

If you stumbled upon this book, I implore you to entertain the idea that it was not by accident. No matter what brought you here, I pray my story will offer you the hope and inspiration that God is longing to provide. May I decrease, and God increase as you reflect on my testimony.

PART ONE

Passion, Purpose, and Pain

I can do all this through Him who gives me strength.
Philippians 4:13

1

Seven Little Words

March 2018

The monotonous drone of the television filled my hospital room, serving as the soundtrack to a test of my patience and faith.

"What's wrong with me, God?"

I had convinced myself that things weren't as bad as they seemed, but now I am afraid.

"God, I need you."

Dr. Willis's entrance interrupted my prayerful thoughts. With no hesitation, he began explaining my test results, but I heard nothing after these seven life-changing words.

"There is nothing we can do for you here."

His jarring words struck me like a freight train barreling toward the intersection of hope and reality. Time moves forward, whether we're ready or not. But in this moment, I felt like Heaven was holding its breath. Fear crept up my spine, tightening every muscle, before reaching my tense jaws and grinding teeth. Dr. Willis's pronouncement left me stunned and gasping for a breath of hope.

Lying there in silence, I clung to my husband, Ralph's, hand as if it were the only solid thing in the room. His grip had steadied me throughout our marriage—in good times and the hardest of times—but tonight was different. We'd waited so long for answers about why my body was failing me—and whether the solid ground under our feet was about to shift forever.

NOTHING WE CAN DO FOR YOU HERE.

Dr. Willis had spoken seven powerful words that shocked my entire nervous system. I tried to listen as he explained my test results, but the words, "Nothing we can do for you here," spun around in my brain like the tumble cycle in a dryer. I was numb. I could not feel my body.

When I finally found my voice, I asked him what this all meant and then strung together eight of the most important words I'd ever put together. "Is there any hope at all for me?"

The journey to this moment left me with more questions than answers. Did the long wait equate to a serious diagnosis, or was I simply overthinking things? Hindsight should have been a glaring red flag. I was moved from the ER to a regular room. The fact that the nurses hadn't reconnected my IV lines and monitors spoke loudly, yet without a word. Scattered thoughts allowed for little rational thinking. Instead, I silently cried out to God, searching for a reality I could hold on to.

Transported to an all too familiar place, I found myself in Grandmother Sadie's hospital room. In her eighties, she battled the debilitating effects of hardening of the arteries, which led to vascular dementia. As a young adult, accompanying my mother on many of her visits to Grandmother's nursing home, Mom's inherent lessons of nurturing and commitment blessed me. The doctors made it clear that the effects of Grandmother's dementia could not be reversed. Prayers were said, and family members visited. My self-prescribed role was supporter to my mother and intercessor for my grandmother.

"Lord, heal my grandmother. You know that she's a strong, Christian woman who loves you. She needs you, and I need her."

This fervent prayer was on a constant loop of faith tempered by desperation as Grandmother's health continued to decline. Her emaciated frame, lost within the bed covers, reminded us just how close she was to meeting her Lord.

After multiple hospital visits, the doctors finally said the words we feared most: *"There's nothing else we can do."* Even though we'd sensed this moment coming, the blow landed hard —like a bomb bursting inside our chests. I carried those words with me as they sent my precious grandmother back to the nursing home to spend her last days.

My beautiful, four-foot-eleven-inch grandmother married the love of her life at the tender age of fourteen. They raised fifteen children and had more grandchildren than even they could count.

As the grandchild who lived nearest Grandmother Sadie, I was blessed to spend time with her regularly after my grandfather died. Grandmother was a quiet, honorable woman of great strength. She faithfully lived the Proverbs 31 attributes of a Christian woman by praying and reading God's Word, caring for her family, and showing kindness everywhere she went. Her

Bible study and church attendance were as predictable as the sunrise and sunset.

She was also the epitome of the old saying, "Dynamite comes in small packages." On more than one occasion, Grandmother and I pushed the limits with my parents. My mind frequently revisits a scene in the field behind her house, where we took turns shooting cans off fence posts. No, we weren't using a real gun—but close. During one of Grandmother's dynamite days, she decided I needed a BB gun and ordered one from her favorite place: the Sears and Roebuck catalog. Mind you, I never asked for a BB gun. Grandmother was living vicariously through me. Watching her squint and aim my shiny new gun felt like God's way of blessing me with an example of her tenacity and playful spirit. He wants us to have some fun in life, and we certainly did.

Walking with Grandmother Sadie remains my most powerful memory of time spent with her. The modest home was on the edge of town, down a blacktop road. Grandmother usually refused rides from my parents or her friends, choosing to walk instead. I joined her every chance I could.

Oh, the powerful life lessons that I learned listening to Grandmother Sadie's wisdom as we navigated that sticky blacktop road. The priceless lessons and moments of laughter were worth the black-stained shoe soles. Even in my youth, these shared walks struck a relevant chord with me because, in the innocence of walking, Grandmother had a higher mission. Every step was one step closer to my relationship with Jesus Christ.

During many of our walks, I asked, "Grandmother, why do you love walking so much?"

Her answer remained consistent. "Because me and God talk things out on my walks."

My young mind was intrigued but confused. Was God visibly walking alongside Grandmother? What did He look like? Did other people driving by see Him? I always had follow-up questions. "Does God talk to you out loud? What does He sound like?"

With a soft chuckle and a smile, she reached for my hand and replied, "Sometimes He does, but mostly He speaks to me through His Word and through people He places on my path."

"What does that mean, Grandmother?"

"The hard part isn't hearing from God. It's being obedient to His Word, just like you obey your parents. Ask God to help you recognize His voice and to be obedient. He wants to walk with you through life. He loves you."

Grandmother reminded me of a song I'd heard at her church about walking with the Lord.

"And He walks with me, and He talks with me,
And He tells me I am His own;
And the joy we share as we tarry there,
None other has ever known."

"I remember that song, Grandmother."

My little heart pounded out of my chest. I always did my best to sing along with her.

After Dr. Willis's staggering words, it was clear I would need to lean harder than ever on my grandmother's lessons.

They would be my anchor as I faced the toughest days of my life. I would also need the strength of the man God gave to me.

I married my soulmate and the most handsome, strongest man I'd ever met. From our first date until four and a half years later, when I walked down the aisle to marry Ralph Porter, every day was verification that he was my person. Standing proudly, yet nervously, at the end of the aisle, tears threatened to spill from his glistening eyes as I approached. The culmination of a year of planning was wrapped up in that moment. Vows and rings were exchanged with shaking hands. Check. The big kiss happened. Check. Then, Ralph took my hand as we turned to face our guests and begin our walk through life together.

Daily walks became integral in solidifying our adulthood. We strolled through our neighborhood as proud new homeowners. These walks helped us connect with our neighbors while also reconnecting us at the end of our workdays. Ralph's work travel often required me to walk solo until his return.

A few months after our marriage in 1980, my precious grandmother was called to her forever home with the Lord. Her passing was as quiet and respectful as she had lived her life. Her death left a hole in my heart that no one else could fill. Tears weren't enough to relieve my grief or replace my connection with my dear grandmother. She began speaking to me from her vantage point in Heaven, encouraging me and assuring me that God was the way.

Our conversations about walking and talking to God bubbled up in my soul during my solo walks. So, this was my opportunity to hear from God and to pour my heart out to Him as well. When the words "There is nothing we can do for you here" were spoken, I knew Jesus was in the room. He had met me every time and walked with me. There was no reason to believe He would fail.

2

Passion, Purpose, and Pain

June 2015

I wanted to get fit, but I needed the camaraderie of working out with a group. My coworker invited me to join her for a program called Fit Camp. After we discussed upping my fitness routine, she assured me I would connect with others at my fitness level, so I got online and provided my information. The moment I clicked submit to register, regret tapped on my shoulder, whispering discouragement.

What are you doing?

You can't keep up with those fitness fanatics.

Maybe you can get your money back.

Even my best attempt at encouraging self-talk didn't extinguish regret's voice.

You can't cut it.

It was time for a serious confidence boost. I needed my daughter, Lauren, and her supportive encouragement.

As our firstborn, Lauren grew up testing the waters of life and our patience, as most young adults do. All the while, she held onto our love as Ralph and I held onto her. Adult Lauren conjures up quiet strength in life's trenches. As I sat staring at the fitness camp's registration page, that was exactly what I needed. My finger hovered above the submit button as I grabbed my phone and texted her.

Me: What was I thinking listening to you, Lauren? I can't do this.

Lauren: Mom. Yes, you can! You're stronger than you think. You've got this!

Me: But what if I'm the oldest one out there?

Lauren's words came back fast and full of the encouragement I needed.

Lauren: So what! Be the oldest and do your best.

Me: Okay! Okay! Here I go! I'll call later if I'm still alive.

She was right. I could do this.

Lauren's joyful, loving reassurance did the trick. I hit the submit icon, and my registration was confirmed. Wearing my new workout shoes, I was cautiously excited and on my way to a healthier, more fit body. (Yes, I'd already bought new shoes because what woman isn't motivated by new shoes?)

After a challenging and embarrassing fitness evaluation on the first day of Fit Camp, I committed to keep going back. For the next two years, my morning routine began at 4:30 a.m. The Fit Campers were friendly and supportive. Many were just like me. Finding my walking tribe was crucial. These were my people. I gained strength from our similarities, and their encouragement was often the one thing that kept me going when my gas tank was empty. We hung out at the back of the pack, clearing a path for the runners. Running wasn't and had never been my jam.

Our tribe was stronger than any of our personal commitments. God formed bonds between us. After all, there are so many places in His Word that make it clear He created us for community rather than solitude. New friends with a common goal, supporting each other, were a timely yet unexpected blessing for me.

Per our coaches, accountability and consistency were key. If not for those 4:30 a.m. "get yourself up" texts, some of us wouldn't have shown up. As a hit-the-alarm and put-your-feet-on-the-floor person, I was usually one of the nagging, Suzy Sunshine texters. My adult children would confirm my Suzy Sunshine status. There was little they despised more than me waking them for school by flipping on their bedroom light and belting out, "Wakey. Wakey Eggs and Bakey!" Like it or not, I was a morning mom.

Challenged and encouraged by our coaches' smiles and tenacity, about fifty of us gathered each morning for Coach Kelly's drill-sergeant-style, no-excuse instructions. Coach Mia, on the other hand, was known for her huge smile and what she called "Mia counts." These counts always meant more reps or miles than she originally called out. She was as tough as Coach Kelly, but she brought the fun, too. No workout ended without her joking around and dancing. Our coaches complemented each other perfectly. They made each workout effective and fun.

My body's gradual transformation spurred me on. The walking, tire flipping, and car pushing were making a difference. I worked out hard and ate healthier, journaling every morsel of food I consumed. The weight came off while my muscle mass increased.

Honoring my body as God's temple breathed new life into me. My time in His Word inspired me as I meditated on these verses:

"Do you not know that your bodies are temples of the Holy Spirit, who is in you, whom you have received from God?" 1 Corinthians 6:19 (NIV)

"So, whether you eat or drink or whatever you do, do it all for the glory of God." 1 Corinthians 10:31 (NIV)

I thanked the Lord for my fitness friends and praised Him for the wisdom of exercising because honoring my temple proved to be a joy. The healthier me was an affirming bonus.

Ralph thought I was crazy for subjecting myself to the extremes that Fit Camp required, but I refused to quit. He supported me and even attended as a guest a few times. We were walking through life with the confidence of children of God, doing our best to take care of ourselves. Overall, life was good.

One day, Lauren called with an unexpected opportunity. She pitched the idea of us doing the 3-Day together. Often referred to as the 3-Day, the Susan G. Komen 3-Day Walk is a sixty-mile walk to raise money for breast cancer research, patient care, and advocacy efforts. Walkers complete twenty miles daily and camp overnight in tents.

My first reaction was more hesitant than anything else. Isn't it that way with many of us when God plants a new idea in our hearts? We're too often quick to dismiss or delay action on the idea, with feeble excuses. I was certainly guilty as charged, so I began my litany of questions to avoid this commitment.

"Are you crazy? Three days of walking all day *and* camping at night?"

Appealing to my ego and competitive nature, Lauren came back with, "Mom, you're killing your workout routine. Plus, this is something we can do as mother and daughter."

In that instant, all hesitation faded.

"Okay, you had me at the mother/daughter argument. I'm in."

She also had me at raising funds for breast cancer—a cause close to my heart after witnessing family members and friends suffer. The scripture from *Galatians 6:2 (NIV)* rose from my heart.

"Carry each other's burdens and in this way, you will fulfill the law of Christ."

This was the season to use my walking passion to benefit others. Christ calls us to responsibility to one another, especially those whose burden is too heavy to carry alone. Sensing a nod from God and Grandmother Sadie, I hopped online and registered.

With the commitment made, our to-do list was short: train, pack, and go. The suggested walking schedule was daunting, but well planned and effective. Fit Camp had me in better shape than I realized. Once I mastered fifteen miles a day, my confidence kicked in, and I was ready.

Walking was the perfect opportunity for me to increase my prayer time. With nothing between me and nature's architecture, walking and talking with God became my bigger motivation. Grandmother Sadie's commitment to "walking and talking with Jesus" now resonated on a deeper level. Stepping away from life's distractions and into a holy space with the Father transformed every day into pure solace. Just as Jesus sought privacy to pray, I longed for quiet time with the Father. The Father wants time with each of His children and waits patiently for us to make space for Him. We are blessed that His patience far exceeds ours.

The day arrived for the 3-Day Walk. Lauren and I showed up prepared, donning pink from head to toe. If we are anything, we are about a theme, hence the feather boas, matching blinged-out walking gear, and all the accessories. During the first day, fellow walkers wasted no time nicknaming us the Mother/Daughter team, and we walked in that designation with love and pride.

As camping novices, we solicited help with erecting our tent. Our camping neighbors were happy to oblige, so we were all set up in no time. Neither the porta-potties nor the shower trucks weakened our determination. We sweated, walked, and sweated some more. Walkers belted out songs as upbeat music pumped motivation through their Bluetooth speakers. We danced along the route, walked arm in arm, and hyped each other up to complete each day's twenty miles. Memories and friendships were made, and tears of struggle and accomplishment were shed before we proudly crossed the finish line.

After the obligatory and expected recovery days, I was back to my usual workout routine. The 3-Day proved to be a life-changing experience. Being surrounded by thousands of strong cancer warriors and supporters with amazing stories of bravery and perseverance was overwhelming, yet inspirational. Listening to their stories of determination and faith awakened a newfound appreciation for my own health and for God's faithfulness and mercy for His children.

Not wanting to forget any memories we'd created, I got busy journaling. Putting pen to paper had always been my favorite way to decompress. Page after page, I documented the adventure Lauren and I had shared. Before closing my journal, my final entry was a commitment to do the walk again the next year.

Time passed in the blink of an eye, and soon, Lauren and I recruited two more walkers to complete our team, and Team Faithful Soles was born. We hyped them up with stories of camaraderie and fun during the 3-Day weekend. Our team was excited and committed.

This time around, though, I struggled to complete my training. Too many days, I had to pause my walks to pray for the strength to finish.

I called out to God:

"What's going on with my body, Lord?"

"I thought you called me to do this."

"Help me finish the mission, Lord."

God met me there as I struggled with frustration and unexpected physical battles. He reminded me that no matter how hard we try, we must admit that we can do nothing without Him. If we call on Him, He will rescue us and strengthen us.

The scripture I meditated on during that time was *John 15:5 (NIV):*

"I am the vine; you are the branches. If you remain in Me, and I in you, you will bear much fruit; apart from Me you can do nothing."

Team Faithful Soles completed our mission, thanking God as we crossed the finish line. Standing there at the closing ceremony rally amid a sea of rain-soaked pinked-out walkers, nothing could take away our gratitude and sense of accomplishment.

After a fitful night of pain, laced with very little sleep, I dreaded the drive home. Something was horribly wrong. Every muscle in my body ached, and my level of fatigue was unlike anything I'd experienced before. I could barely stay awake to drive. I'm talking about fatigue on steroids. Out of desperation, I stopped at a convenience store to rest for a few minutes. While there, I called out to the Lord:

"Oh God, what's happening right now?"

"Please don't leave me."

"Get me home, God."

Then I called Ralph. He wouldn't be home when I got there, because he was away on business. I was grateful that he stayed on the phone with me. He rode shotgun, keeping me company via his phone as I reluctantly got back on the road. He listened to every groan and prayer as I made the rest of the drive home.

I repeated the words, "Please, Lord, get me home safely. I'm afraid of what's happening to my body. Don't leave me."

With God and my husband, I was able to stay alert, feeling supported and safe the whole way.

Last year's 3-Day recovery was challenging, but after a week of rest, I was back to normal. This year, after hours of bed rest and pain meds, excruciating pain in muscles I didn't even know I had, awakened me. It didn't feel like a truck ran over me; it felt as if one had crushed my muscles and drained every ounce of my strength. My sweat-drenched pajamas were a strong indication that this year's recovery was promised a more intense battle.

My high pain tolerance and independence had gotten me through two childbirths and multiple surgeries. I couldn't imagine why this situation would be any different. I could handle this. I tried to convince myself the pain was just a result of turning a year older, but my body told a different story. I was crawling to the bathroom. Something wasn't right. I knew it in the depths of my soul.

PART TWO
Walking Through Change

"To everything there is a season, and a time to every purpose under the heaven."
Ecclesiastes 3:1

3

Whose Body Is This?

Ralph returned the next morning. As he watched me fight my way to the bathroom, his expression said what my body had been trying to tell me. The comfort of his hug triggered my tears. In horror, he listened through my sobs as I recounted my pain and fear of the last twenty-four hours. The lines on his forehead showed his concern as I described my bathroom ritual from the night before. Scooting to the edge of the bed and sliding onto the floor were the first steps of the process. Crying in pain, cautiously crawling to connect with my dresser, then furniture surfing the rest of the way into the bathroom was the rest of the plan and my last resort. He later told me just how jarring and frightening it was seeing me barely strong enough to move.

By afternoon, with Ralph's help, we joined other patients in our doctor's waiting room. Per my natural response to new situations, I used the moments when the pain relievers went into effect to research my symptoms. This led to a plethora of speculation. After checking off eight out of ten symptoms, the most logical conclusion was that I had fibromyalgia.

Unaware of my actions, I sat wringing my hands and

fidgeting in my seat. Ralph sensed my nervousness and reached for my hand. If my prediction was true, I would need his strength and hope more than ever before. I wasn't in this alone. God and Ralph had walked me through Grandmother's illness and death, plus so many other trials. I reminded myself of these blessings and thanked God for His faithfulness.

One of our best lines of defense in times of trouble is remembering God's prior victories in our lives. He's been with each one of us every step of the way, whether or not we recognized His presence. No trial that we've made it through was because of our own power. God deserves all the glory. We must also remind ourselves through His Word that He is always at work on our behalf.

Dr. Strickland stepped into the room, and I began rattling off my list of symptoms. My anxiety heightened as he scooted closer to me on his stool. We'd had many conversations in this exact examining room, but I'd never experienced the foreboding weight that I recognized in his eyes. Halfway through my litany, he reached out and touched my shoulder. My heart spoke louder than the voiceless words I held onto, and my breath hitched momentarily.

"Here's what I know for sure after treating you for years, Pam. You have a Type A personality. You're an overachiever, a people-pleaser, and you're burned out. All of that makes you a classic candidate for fibromyalgia, or fibro, as we refer to it. The most effective way to get a diagnosis is to run tests that will rule out other possibilities or widen our search for answers."

As I fought to hold back my tears, every aching muscle in

my body doubled its intensity. Just as I suspected, my pain receptors had gone into overdrive, which explained my constant and higher level of pain. The crazy part is that if I had known the impact Fibro would have on my life in years to come, I would have morphed into a puddle of tears and desperation right there in his office. Naïveté wasn't necessarily a bad thing in this case. In fact, it was exactly the protection I needed that day.

"No!" I softly yelled, if there is such a thing. Gripping the metal chair arm tighter, I continued.

"The little I know about Fibro and how it robs people of normalcy scares me. I don't want this to be true, but...schedule those tests and get me some answers. I can't go on like this."

Although Ralph will attest to the fact that I love being right, it was far from true in this case. I would have been happy to take an L for the loss on this one. My plunge into the deep end of fibromyalgia research and support groups, including sufferers' testimonials, continued, as did my constant pain. The results enlightened me while at the same time, heightening my anxiety about my future.

After extensive bloodwork, imaging, and interrogation about my symptoms and my lifestyle, Ralph and I found ourselves in a familiar waiting scenario. Would life change in an instant with one diagnosis, or was my pain temporary—something that required a simple solution?

Our wait was brief. With other possible explanations ruled out by negative test results, Dr. Strickland's diagnosis was confirmed. I did in fact have fibromyalgia. An uncelebrated win for me.

Doing his best not to overwhelm me, Dr. Strickland presented day one of Fibro 101, a masterclass in layman's terms, including symptoms and suggestions for the immediate future. He wrote prescriptions for my headaches and lack of sleep, with the understanding that I could request medication for other symptoms as they manifested. Our drive home was shrouded in the silence of disbelief and concern.

This diagnosis would be life-altering for both of us. Ralph married an energetic, self-motivated woman, but was now forced to watch his wife unravel before his eyes. I had built a life as a fun, hardworking, helpful wife, who now, due to an incurable illness, faced unforeseen limitations.

An ex-coworker of mine was the only person I knew who lived with Fibro. Desperate for some perspective beyond what I was finding on the internet, I called her. She was kind enough to gift me with her time and her compassion. I've always said that much can be resolved or at least quietened in our minds by having a good visit with a real friend.

As Beth invited me into her world of chronic illness, my appreciation for her perseverance and faith grew exponentially. This woman juggled the rigor of teaching kindergarten, along with managing a family, an active church life, and a busy social life.

Beth was that friend whose light entered the room ahead of her. Her beaming smile and boisterous laughter put everyone at ease. Meanwhile, Fibro was doing what it does best: hiding in plain sight, wreaking havoc on her body and her mind. I had no idea the level of pain she dealt with daily. Anytime I dropped in on her class, I came away in awe of her joy and creativity, despite her condition.

One takeaway from our conversation was that Meryl Streep-level acting skills are a prerequisite for most chronic illness sufferers. Downplaying symptoms is easier than attempting to explain their devastating impact. Pretending to be okay while fighting constant pain is one of the reasons we in the Fibro community call ourselves warriors.

"Putting on my game face" meant pasting on my best fake smile, enhanced by bright lipstick, to camouflage my physical and emotional pain. It's yet another reason fibromyalgia is exhausting on every level. Patients suddenly find themselves tasked with helping family and friends feel comfortable, when instead it should be the other way around. We spend precious energy pushing ourselves beyond our limits or hiding our pain because those around us are uncomfortable when they don't know how to react.

Beth shared a wealth of knowledge from her own walk down Fibro Road. Because of this new lifestyle that I was being forced to navigate, her last two bits of advice will forever be with me.

"I can't express strongly enough how this illness affects your relationships with your partner, your family, and your friends," Beth said. "My number one bit of advice is to never feel guilty about your condition. You didn't cause it.

"Second, no matter what others may think about your illness, you know your own truth. Respect your body and live in your truth, not the world's."

Even though the information Beth shared was intimidating, knowing I wasn't alone was comforting. That someone who really got it was available by phone or text lifted my spirits. Walking away from our visit, my stride was stronger, and my head was a little higher.

Our diagnoses merged over invaluable information and coffee that day. Thanking God for the love and support of a friend, I went to bed with this scripture on my mind.

"A friend loves at all times, and a brother is born for a time of adversity." Proverbs 17:17 (NIV)

Being thrown into the deep end of a chronic illness is a brutal baptism. Paralyzed by the fear of the unknown is, however, nowhere close to the daily reality of living with fibromyalgia. I needed Ralph, Beth, and my doctor as my floaties.

4

Seasons Change

As someone who has seen God's unseen hand work things out for my good, I have faith in God but remain awestruck every time He demonstrates His mercy by working things out for me. His matchless portion of love and faithfulness was positioning me for the coming season.

God's work behind the scenes of my current season was revealed to me in His timing. This scripture repeatedly jumped off the page during my Bible study time, reminding me of His promise:

"We have hope as an anchor for the soul, firm and secure. It enters the inner sanctuary behind the curtain, where our forerunner, Jesus, has entered on our behalf." Hebrews 6:19-20 (NIV)

A significant part of my identity had been tied to teaching, but it was time to embark on a new path. Education had experienced cyclical changes throughout my career, and I'd hung onto that rollercoaster, making the most of my ride, until burnout brought the coaster to a screeching halt. Prayer and discussions about our financial future, along with thoughts on how to fill my free time, were frequent topics in our home for months. Heeding God's urging and my blown motivational fuse, I tendered my resignation after thirty-five years in the classroom. Walking into the next season of my life, I trusted God to provide and guide me.

For one year, I was blessed to volunteer with a local philanthropic organization whose impact extended far beyond our community. Serving, organizing, and doing mission work all opened the door for a beautiful opportunity for me to bless others. Understanding Fibro's signals and knowing when to rest or compensate was a herculean learning curve. Some days manifested themselves in shorter hours or staying home to rest. Other times, it resembled more frequent breaks and choosing lighter job assignments to avoid exhaustion and throbbing pain. Walking a path laden with unexpected new symptoms, while helping others, was a blessing and a lesson that would serve me well on my next journey.

As life settles into an easy pace, something invariably disrupts our peace with an unexpected sharp turn. Such was the morning that my mom told us that her husband, Reverend Williams, had experienced an aneurysm and was rushed to the hospital. My heart went out to him and my mom. Yes, they were the pastor and the pastor's wife, but in this crisis, they were any couple battling an illness.

As I threw clothes into a bag, I contemplated how my body would withstand the stress of this situation. I desperately wanted to support Mom, but I was concerned about my physical and mental ability to do so. With medications packed and prayers spoken between Ralph and me, I challenged the speed limit every minute of the three-hour drive to the hospital. Rev.

Williams' condition was serious. His children agreed to take turns staying overnight with him to give Mom some rest.

Once I got her settled at home each night, an Epsom salt bath was my sanctuary. The Holy Spirit met me there, offering revival and strength to help Mom walk her husband home with love and faith. After several arduous days and nights filled with family, prayers, and decisions, Rev. Williams went to be with the Lord. Yet again, God had walked with me and the family as our source of peace, as *2 Thessalonians 3:16 (NIV)* assured us:

"Now may the Lord of peace himself give you peace at all times and in every way. The Lord be with all of you."

Uncomfortable with living alone in her eighties, Mom chose to move in with us, without the coercion we had dreaded. Household dynamic changes were expected, but we trusted God to walk us through those transitions with grace.

Ralph and I embraced having Mom live with us, despite the questioning comments from some of Ralph's friends who couldn't fathom having their mother-in-law live with them. He was not, however, deterred, but instead, accepted the mission with love and strength. We were raised to respect family and to live a Godly life, just as the Bible tells us in *Exodus 20:12 (NIV):*

"Honor your father and your mother, so that you may live long in the land the Lord your God is giving you."

If you are alone facing a similar situation, trust that God will not only provide strength, but also His comfort on the toughest days. None of us is truly alone when we call on God. He is what we need Him to be in our lives if we only ask.

Mom insisted on one condition upon moving in: if or when

she needed nursing care, we would move her to a facility that could provide it. She did not want us to become her nurses.

Soon after settling in, she adopted the nickname "roommate" to define her independent role in our home. Her self-discipline and moderately good health meant she insisted on handling as many daily chores as possible. Initially, my caregiving role included chauffeuring her to appointments and shopping trips, as well as being her jigsaw puzzle buddy.

One of Mom's favorite pastimes was her puzzles. She took pride in being able to complete one thousand-piece puzzles in record time. Soon after she moved in, we bought her a puzzle table with drawers to organize the pieces. She was as excited as a child on Christmas morning. Mom invited us to join her at the puzzle table daily. Ralph wasn't a big puzzle fan, but he searched the board with a smile to please his mother-in-law. We spent hours searching for elusive pieces, as well as for life's big answers, during conversations around the table. Mom's puzzle table became our altar. As her arthritic fingers struggled to grasp puzzle pieces—and often our hands—she ministered to us, offering biblical teaching and life lessons.

Every evening's puzzle time ended the same way. Mom and I would hug for as long as either of us needed, knowing we were creating precious memories together. Moments like these temporarily took away the sting of living with an incurable chronic illness. On the harder days, when caregiving brought pain and worry, God blessed Ralph and me through Mom's love and Christian witness. Faith carried each of us into the next season of our lives.

5

Grief Isn't Just for Death

Wrapping my head around my new life was akin to being pushed into the deep end of the pool before swimming lessons. Just keeping my head above water was a challenge for which I was unprepared. Even though Fibro battled to control my day-to-day decisions, I refused to relinquish my grip on the One who was ultimately in control. *Psalm 37:23 (KJV)* could be found scribbled in my Bible margins, as well as on sticky notes on my bathroom mirror. I read this scripture repeatedly throughout my day as I grieved my old life:

"The steps of a good man are ordered by the Lord, and He delighteth in his way."

Maintaining my mental health wasn't always easy. Many people don't realize it, but like death, illness causes grief. I'd lost my past life and had to make adjustments in the plans I had for my future.

Walking with God comforted me while also requiring deeper trust. He guided me through individual steps that were lessons in patience and humility. I struggled with asking for or accepting help during my toughest days. God opened my mind and heart to the possibility of allowing others to bless me and to receive their own blessing from their acts of kindness. Ultimately, obedience was the key to handling each day's fresh dose of grief.

Making plans was often frustrating and futile when my ability to follow through with those plans could change in an instant, because the day or even the hour was fueled by pain, fatigue, brain fog, and more. Meanwhile, people saw the same person I always was. Letting others down and missing out on exciting things were reasons enough for me to continue grieving my old life. Friends and family saw the same me, but God saw the invisible illness that silently controlled my every move. No one would choose to be diagnosed with anything, but at least people understand what you're going through when the illness manifests itself physically. This isn't a cry for sympathy. It's a plea for the same respect any visible illness would garner. The unbelief and dismissal by others play a major part in Fibro warriors' grief. I remain convinced that everything we experience in life is a lesson from God. Grief is a tough one.

Living with fibromyalgia remains a mystery to most of the world's population. We are often perceived as lazy, attention-seeking hypochondriacs. Sufferers must find ways to quiet that noise and focus on their own self-care. Trust me. The last thing any of us wants is the attention garnered from the focus on our limitations. A common phrase in the chronic illness world is, "We aren't faking being ill. We're faking being okay."

For me, dealing with my new diagnosis twenty-four hours a day, three hundred sixty-five days of the year was a bigger challenge than caregiving. Dr. Strickland did what he could to address my individual symptoms. This led to an unbelievable cache of prescription pills that filled a large Ziploc bag. I never envisioned managing an oversized pill organizer that resembled one on a nursing home medicine cart. The biggest issue was that the myriad of side effects were often worse than my original symptoms. It's been said, "Sometimes, you have to pick your poison." Desperately, I tried to turn off the question that kept resurfacing.

"What would my life be like in the decades to come?"

Feeling misunderstood and judged, social groups dedicated to fibromyalgia warriors became my respite. While I appreciated the concern of those closest to me, it was equally exhausting dealing with the questions and invalid comments. It wasn't their fault that they didn't understand my condition. Neither did I. Social media group members were my tribe. They understood.

Family and friends warned me not to go down the rabbit hole of such groups. They worried I would land smack dab in the middle of depression. To be honest, some of the posts triggered thoughts about my future with a chronic illness. Moderation was the key to keeping myself above the Fibro pool's surface, where support could be found.

So many nights I lay awake in pain and loneliness, crying out to God, as tears stained my pillow. My normal level of support from God held no comparison to how much I needed His strength in this battle. He listened lovingly as I ranted and questioned Him. He met me in quiet moments with assurance and instruction. Every call for help was met with an invitation for a deeper relationship with Him. The pull on my soul brought me to a place of more consistent study of God's Word. The pages of my Bible wore the tears of my heart as I prayed and studied, but every example of His power and faithfulness helped strengthen me for the fight ahead.

Having a trusted therapist was also a key component in my self-care regimen. Admitting my truths in a safe, impartial environment opened my soul and my mind even further. Typically, I held my feelings close to my heart and drew inward in hard times like these. When I recognized that most of my world included hard "No's" and "Before Fibro," I needed God and therapy. By no means would I recommend therapy over prayer. The two can coexist. God can place qualified professionals in our lives as a part of His overall support plan.

To outsiders, this may seem overdramatic and unnecessary, but if you haven't had control over your body stripped away in the blink of an eye, please allow me and other Fibro warriors added grace. Our worlds have been upended.

One of mine and Ralph's "I used to" hobbies before my Fibro diagnosis was hiking. It was yet another way for us to walk together. Plus, sharing time in nature was a beautiful confirmation of God's handiwork and His power.

Ralph had an exemplary career in agricultural sales that wasn't by accident, but rather by fervent dedication and hard work. He had the same level of commitment to his job as he did to our family. Work trips were a requirement for him to maintain his respected position in his company and with his valued customers. Unfortunately, that meant time apart for us. I appreciated the qualities that he exhibited in every facet of his life, but I also recognized the toll that his career took on him personally. He had far less time for friends or church and civic commitments. For this and other reasons, our hiking adventures were valued times to unplug and reconnect as a couple.

One of Ralph's coworkers recommended the Bataan Death March in New Mexico. Upon researching it, we learned this march was to honor and commemorate the American and Filipino soldiers who were forced to march sixty-five miles through the Philippines in 1942.

We packed, drove, and checked in at the starting location. Being surrounded by wounded warriors and other veterans weighed on my spirit as I pondered the stories and sacrifices they bore along this trail. Tears, war chants, and words of encouragement filled the air that day. Experiencing the physical hike paled in comparison to their struggle.

Bitten by the hiking bug, our next trek was in Big Bend National Park. We'd visited the park multiple times but had never hiked it before. After an early breakfast and a stop by the ranger station, including a warning about bears and mountain lions, we were on our way. Admittedly, that little warning tamped down my enthusiasm a bit, but we forged ahead. Hours went by, but our bodies and spirits remained strong. A map check at the mountain's summit showed that we'd veered off the trail miles back. With sunset threatening, we had one mission: avoiding mountain lions and bears on the way back to our cabin. Rounding the last corner of the trail, with darkness looming, the shadow of our cabin welcomed us.

Once again, we'd successfully navigated our newfound passion. Then Fibro said, "No." All future hiking plans were put on hold. With much reluctance, we accepted that Big Bend was our last hike. The nagging memories of things I did before Fibro bring on sadness and even tears. I had no choice but to accept this limited lifestyle that was thrust upon me, but I didn't have to like it. Yes, I was grateful to be more mobile than some, but I also understood that some people weren't as active as I was before my diagnosis. This made the impact of my lifestyle loss heavier and more difficult to endure every day. There are very few moments when absolutely nothing on my body hurts, or nothing is uncontrollably spinning in my mind. It's a lot with no end in sight.

My Fit Camp friends from my workout days continued reaching out to check on me after Fibro forced me to drop out of the camp. I missed them terribly and wanted to get back to working out, but Fibro said, "No." I always enjoyed spending hours browsing boutiques and bookstores. But Fibro said, "No." Ralph and I loved new adventures and quiet getaways, but Fibro said, "No." The word "No" was synonymous with fibromyalgia, at least in my world. "I used to... before fibro" became a daily reference in my journal entries, as well as to invitations I was forced to decline.

January 10, 2017

Dear Journal,

Another day, after another fitful night, desperate for sleep. A night filled with achy joints that had me flopping around in bed like a fish out of water, seeking a comfortable position, for even a single moment. By six o'clock in the morning, I relented and tried sitting upright on the couch. No sleep, but time for journaling. These pages hold my deepest thoughts, and lately they seemed to be mostly about my health and lifestyle changes.

I'm so tired of saying "No" to what used to be automatic yeses. I miss my Fit Camp friends. Meeting them for coffee after they work out just isn't the same as working out together. Their conversations and inside jokes leave me feeling left out. I fight tears as I sip my coffee. Their attempts to draw me into the conversation with questions about my life make me uncomfortably aware that my answers will sound negative and whiny. That's when my new role as an actress kicks in. With my biggest fake smile, I assure them I'm hanging in there. What I want to do is scream, "I'm miserable most of the time, and I'm tired of it!"

Today's a new day. May it be tolerable and a step closer to acceptance of my "No's." Until tomorrow, blessings and love.

My journal became my lifeline and part of my therapy. Writing my innermost thoughts freed up space in my mind and provided a daily bonfire for my frustration.

After rereading months of journal entries filled with negativity, I knew it was time to flip the script. Reframing my thoughts about my situation meant writing about my new lifestyle from the perspective of "Yes." Visually, the "No's" had to go. Now, I thought and wrote from a place of acceptance. Yes, I planned my activities based on the amount of physical activity and mental stimulation involved. Yes, I took more breaks. Yes, I depended on Ralph to drive on long trips and at night. Yes, guilt rose in me when I was unable to help in group situations.

Yes, I canceled plans at the last minute if my Fibro flared up. Yes, I parked closer to public buildings. My yeses came from a place of deeper acceptance and hope in God for a cure. After all, He can do absolutely anything.

Yes, I use my handicap placard on particularly tough days. I can attest to the fact that the world is not sensitive to invisible illnesses. I've been glared at and told to move my car out of a handicap space, even though I have a legal placard.

On a particularly tough day, I had no choice but to run a few errands. After circling the store parking lot, the available spaces near the entrance were handicapped spots. It would have taken Herculean effort for me to walk from the back of the lot, so I pulled into one of the handicapped spaces and placed my placard on the mirror. As soon as I locked my door and began painfully making my way toward the store, a woman yelled to me from across the row.

"Hey, lady! You don't need that space. You need to move!"

The glare on her face spoke louder than her words. Remembering my childhood home training, I smiled politely.

"Not all health issues are visible," I replied.

The lady walked away after rolling her eyes in frustration. I knew that my struggle to reach the store's front door was far more frustrating, but arguing or trying to explain my condition would have been futile.

None of us knows what others may be going through. I do my best to remember the Golden Rule from my childhood days in Sunday School, found in *Luke 6:31 (NIV).*

"Do to others as you would have them do to you."

Imagine walking around every day feeling like you have the flu, partial dementia, arthritis, cataracts, migraines, gastric issues, full-body inflammation, scent, sight, and crowd sensitivity, and more. All this time, you appear perfectly normal. Being told "you can do it" became a trigger, rather than encouragement. I was desperate for them to understand.

Some of my other trigger phrases are:

"But you don't look sick."

"Just get more sleep."

"Can't they fix that?"

"Just exercise."

"Is fibromyalgia even real?"

"I had that once, but it went away in a few days."

"Seriously, it can't be that bad."

"Do you still have that fibromyalgia thing going on?"

If I had a dollar for every time someone has shared one of those comments, I would be a millionaire. I would also still struggle with daily Fibro symptoms. As a mom, visions of happiness with my family held a prominent space in my mind. Would my body be functional enough for me to take part in the lives of our children and hopefully grandchildren in the future?

PART THREE
Walking with Family

"And over all these virtues put on love, which binds them all together in perfect unity."
Colossians 3:14 (NIV)

6

Meet the Parents

Our introduction to Lauren's fiancé, Quentin, was at a party celebrating her brother, Ryan, and his fiancée, Caitlin. As everyone celebrated the happy couple, Lauren walked into the room unassumingly, while Quentin brought the party as soon as he entered. From our vantage point, we noticed his contagious smile and outgoing personality as we watched him hold his own in a room full of strangers, while still being attentive to Lauren. Her apprehension about introducing a boyfriend to the family could not be hidden behind her bright smile. We observed Lauren watching Quentin with love and support. Things were off to a good start.

Quentin made his way to us. After handshakes and hugs, we slipped into an easy camaraderie, laughing together and joking. Smiles of approval from her brother, future sister-in-law, and us were Lauren's cue to relax and have fun. Quentin had passed the first test with confidence and ease.

No one outside our family understood what a defining moment this was for Lauren. From childhood through young adulthood, she had always been a private person. Family and friends knew her as someone who only opened up to people once she felt completely comfortable. That trait carried into our relationship with her during the parent–teen years. We often heard her whispering on the phone to friends about boys she liked, yet we never received any details beyond what drifted through a closed bedroom door.

Lauren frequently joked that Ralph's perceived military and police officer presence created a barrier for potential boyfriends, not to mention any chance of them meeting us. We weren't trying to scare anyone away; we simply wanted the best for her.

Before we knew it, a "meet the family" get-together was scheduled for Quentin's family and ours. We exchanged funny stories about Quentin and Lauren while creating new bonds. Ralph and I left with warmed hearts and a glimpse of God's goodness in Lauren's life. God was revealing glimpses of His work in our children's lives.

Quentin's job often took him to West Texas, and he had grown comfortable enough to break up the long drive by staying with us. On this visit, after dinner and watching a little football, I headed down the hallway to bed. Halfway there, I heard Quentin say to Ralph, "I want to talk to you about something important."

I froze, my heart pounding. *Is this what I think it is?*

Leaning against the wall, trembling, I listened as Quentin began.

"I love your daughter, and I would appreciate your blessing to ask her to

marry me."

He kept talking, but I couldn't hear anything beyond that

first sentence. My thoughts swirled with anticipation. Would Ralph give him a serious talk or lighten the moment with a joke? This was huge for both of us, but especially for Ralph, the potential father of the bride.

At last, Ralph responded, "Pam and I have watched your relationship grow, so this isn't a complete surprise. We're happy that both of you have found your life partners. Meeting your family and recognizing similar values added to our confidence in your relationship. So, yes, you have our permission and our blessing."

Hearing Ralph's simple but beautiful response brought tears to my eyes and joy to my soul. God had walked with Lauren through joy and pain. Bringing Quentin and her together was a testimony of His protection and faithfulness in her life. After a celebratory hug and speculations about the proposal and wedding, Ralph and I succumbed to our exhaustion and slept with hearts full of gratitude for God's goodness.

One of the most powerful blessings parents can give their children is prayer for Christian spouses who will walk with them and encourage their faith journey. While adult children may prioritize other qualities, Godliness should be number one. With Him at the center of a marriage, security and strength abound. A threefold cord of husband, wife, and God woven together in faith is not easily broken. We rested in the assurance that our prayers were being answered.

Having something joyful to divide my focus was a welcome respite from searching for Fibro coping strategies. My new role as mother of the bride was one I'd planned for with the intensity of an Olympic athlete. Now, my sole concern was whether my body would sustain me in this new role, full of planning and excitement.

I prayed, "Lord, please give me strength. Don't let my health situation be a distraction in this time of happiness and love."

7
Surprise!

Quentin's Aunt Angie and I threw ourselves into his complex proposal plans. Because we lived closer than his parents, it made sense for us to carry out Quentin's vision, and we were determined to make it perfect. For me, that meant runs to Hobby Lobby, long nights of cutting, gluing, and hauling supplies when my body was begging me to stop. Fibromyalgia made every task heavier, but I persevered.

Most evenings ended the same way: me at the kitchen table with sore muscles and tired hands, Angie and I texting and Mom nearby, keeping our spirits lifted. Each ribbon tied, each decoration finished, symbolized a small offering of love for the couple and the life they were about to begin.

It was nearly two in the morning, and I was on the kitchen floor wrestling with a plastic shower curtain and colored duct tape. My body ached, my hands trembled, but I was determined to finish the oversized Tic-Tac-Toe board for the party.

Mom sat at the table, keeping me company with stories of her days as a fifth-grade teacher. With a soft exhale, she slipped down to the floor beside me.

"Here, let me help," she insisted, despite my protests. Together, we lined up the tape, our laughter echoing in the quiet house.

Once the grid was completed, I was ready to collapse into bed, but Mom wasn't done. She handed me a Frisbee with a playful smile on her face. "We made the game. Now we've got to test it."

So, there we were—me battling exhaustion and pain, and Mom with her stubborn determination—tossing frisbees across the kitchen in the middle of the night. She beat me easily, and when we finished our game, I hugged her tightly, knowing how rare and fleeting moments like this could be.

Fibromyalgia tries to take so much from me—strength, energy, ease—but that night it couldn't touch the joy of laughing with my mom. I was reminded of how God gives us joy in the most unexpected places and times. Such was the case at two o'clock in the morning, as we shared so much more than a game on the kitchen floor.

On the morning of the trip, Ralph loaded my car with decorations, games, and enough Hobby Lobby bags to make it look like I moonlighted as an event planner. Before I left, he gave me that serious look—the one that meant *be careful*—and reminded me to pull over and call him if I needed him. I nodded, even as nerves tightened in my chest. Fibromyalgia makes even a short drive unpredictable. As I pulled away, I whispered a prayer, trusting that God had carried me through harder days.

When Angie and I arrived at the house, Quentin filled us in

on the final details of his plan. Lauren thought they were helping his realtor with "marketing photos" for the website, completely unaware that Quentin had already closed on the home. Between his secret late-night moving sessions and his conveniently timed LASIK surgery, which was designed to keep her busy with his recovery, he had covered every angle.

That left the decorating to us. Angie and I unpacked supplies, laughing as we worked, while Quentin texted us instructions from his post-surgery bed across town. He had even installed security cameras and delighted in using the house's speaker system to tease us whenever we moved something out of place. More than once, his voice boomed through the empty rooms, making us jump out of our skin before collapsing in laughter.

Despite the fun, every step, every lift, every trip up the stairs pushed my body past the brink. Still, the joy of preparing for this milestone outweighed the discomfort. Each banner we hung and each table we arranged stitched love into the fabric of Lauren and Quentin's love story. By the time we finished, the house was glowing with anticipation.

"It's perfect," Quentin said. Even through the phone screen, his emotional response was evident. "Thank you both. I'm nervous now."

"You have nothing to be nervous about," Angie and I assured him, though my heart was racing with its own nerves. All we could do was pray that the moment would unfold just as beautifully as he hoped. With every detail planned and executed, I knew keenly that God was the true author of Quentin and Lauren's love story.

The next day, one by one, family and friends slipped into the house. Cars were hidden down the block. There were excited whispers that my teacher's instinct wanted to shush, but I was just as giddy. My heart pounded as Quentin's text interrupted my thoughts: We're almost there.

We pressed close together, barely breathing. The front door opened. Lauren stepped inside, her eyes falling first on the posters we held—each one bearing a word: Will You Marry Me?

The look on her face was priceless. Shock, joy, disbelief. And then, as Quentin dropped to one knee, pure love. Lauren's face was a picture I'll never forget. When she said "yes," the house erupted with cheers. As the two of them sealed their engagement with a kiss, my eyes went straight to Mom. Watching her witness her granddaughter's proposal with tears streaming down her face was a priceless treasure that I'll hold in my heart forever.

The rest of the night was a blur of music, games, a crawfish boil, backyard laughter, and the sparkle of Lauren's ring glistening in the lights. I smiled through every minute, even as my body screamed. By the time we slipped away, I was slathering on pain relief lotion, my muscles aching from hours of pushing far past my limits.

But here's the thing, fibromyalgia may tax my body, but it cannot steal my joy. That night reminded me that sometimes love is worth the pain. I went to bed exhausted but also overflowing with gratitude.

I whispered a prayer of thanks for the strength to witness my child's happiness and for the reminder that God provides the daily manna I need. Not enough for tomorrow, not enough for the wedding planning—just enough for that day. I rested in the promise that He would meet again tomorrow with a fresh blessing of manna.

8
Faith Runs Deep

New day. New mom-ism or adventure. What would today bring? Mom woke up in a good mood every day with a new idea. It was comforting to know that she was happy and still thinking clearly. We packed for an overnight stay at her house in Dallas, which served as our base for medical and business appointments.

After three hours on the highway, we stepped through her front door into several inches of water that swallowed and soaked our shoes. Water covered the floor in every room, overwhelming both of us—especially Mom. Her emotional and mental state took precedence over her flooded house. Once I had her settled in a chair on the front porch, I started making calls. The insurance company and a restoration team arrived within the hour.

The house flooding coincided with Hurricane Harvey's assault on the South Texas coastline, so North Texas hotels were premium real estate. Lauren worked for a major hotel chain. Using her perks, we were able to book rooms throughout the Dallas-Fort Worth area. The problem was that each hotel stay lasted a few days before we had to move on to the next one.

Mom's pace was slower, and her strength waned. Watching her carefully grip the stair rails and need frequent naps tugged at my heart—not just for the vibrant Mom I'd always known, but also because my own Fibro body had started echoing those same small compensations.

As we jokingly compared our struggles with stubborn joints, Mom recognized the cost I was paying for pushing myself too far. In the quiet of mornings and evenings, she could be found on her knees in prayer for my condition. Some of her prayers resulted in my physical relief, while other prayers were steeped in faith lessons on God's timing. Either way, I was blessed by a praying Mom.

For those who aren't fortunate enough to have a praying mother on this side of Heaven, do not be discouraged. This is where plugging into a spiritual community can be God's way of blessing you with mighty prayer warriors. Connect with a small group or one of the many seasoned church mothers at your church. These women have witnessed and experienced life's joys and trials, as well as God's hand in the midst of it all. Allow God to minister to you through them.

Watching Mom kneel beside hotel beds each night to call on Jesus, just as Grandmother Sadie had taught her, humbled me. The Holy Spirit led me to join her at the bedside in prayer. With hands clasped, we established a powerful nightly routine that blessed us both.

I was thankful for the Christian legacy woven throughout generations of my family. I found joy and gratitude in 2 Timothy

1:5 (NIV) where Paul honors Timothy's faith and his legacy inherited from past generations:

"I am reminded of your sincere faith, which lived in your grandmother Lois and in your mother Eunice and, I am persuaded, now lives in you also."

When all repairs were completed, the Dallas house was one thing restored, not the most important one. God had calmed the waters of our hearts and minds and built a stronger bridge of faith between Mom and me.

PART FOUR
Walking with God

"The Lord makes firm the steps of the one who delights in him;
though he may stumble, he will not fall,
for the Lord upholds him with his hand."
Psalm 37:23 (NIV)

9

Preparation and Perseverance

I know very few brides or mothers of the bride who don't want to lose weight for wedding photos. Wanting to look my best, I resorted to a weight-loss specialist suggested by a friend. Hormonal changes added to chronic illness meant limiting workouts to avoid more harm than good. I convinced myself that even if the weight loss was temporary, the photos would look good. Vanity won out.

Per his orders regarding any changes, I sought approval from Dr. Strickland. With the benefits and risks defined, he restricted me to a three-month plan. Respecting the fact that this plan wasn't sustainable for me, I strictly followed both doctors' orders and lost thirty pounds. My new goal was maintenance, with no more weight-loss drugs.

Lauren worked and went to school full-time, while full retirement freed me to help her with wedding plans. Having Mom in our home added to the excitement. She begged to help in any way she could. Doing my best to find simple jobs for her, every sealed envelope and tied bow was a blessing of love and support.

Unfortunately, with every glittered vase and tiny cutout, the intensity of my fibro joint and muscle pain, headaches, and brain fog increased. Through gritted teeth and determination, the projects asked more of me than I could do. I began taking a prescribed muscle relaxer, as directed, to increase my productivity. The meds helped, but my health rapidly declined. Weight was shedding off me, despite ending the weight loss plan several months earlier. Battling for strength resembled furniture surfing for support.

Despite these changes, I pressed on, concerned but even more determined. My attempts at sounding upbeat and strong may have worked with Lauren, long distance, but Ralph and Mom witnessed the extreme changes in my body and continually expressed concern, to no avail. This was my only daughter's wedding. I was willing to risk my health to bring her vision to life.

As time passed, Ralph could no longer ignore my weak attempt at normalcy. He was firm with his suggestion. "You need to see what's going on with you, Pam."

My stubborn streak went into overdrive, with my heels dug in. "I promise to see any doctor, anywhere, as soon as this wedding is over."

With pleading eyes, Ralph shook his head. "You'll never make it to the wedding at this rate, babe."

Yet again, there was no convincing me. The feeling in the depths of my soul that something was seriously wrong became the driving force for me to complete all the wedding projects. If this was the last thing I did, I could rest in the fact that I had contributed to both of our children's wedding dreams.

Meanwhile, my frustration grew as the necessity to rework crafts and seating charts, plus my uber-organized binder that was now an explosion of sticky notes and chaos, all became thorns in my side. Blaming my confusion on Fibro brain fog was a viable excuse until it literally wasn't anymore.

Even though retirement had blessed me with opportunities to bless others, my new lifestyle meant not being around my coworkers daily. So, when the day came for Quentin and Lauren's wedding shower, I stared at my rail-thin body. Lines on my face and dark circles under my eyes were just a few extra gifts from the declining numbers on the bathroom scale. Would my coworkers and friends notice, or could I keep the focus solely on Lauren? My best attempt at a makeover would have to be enough.

Walking into a house filled with friends, family, and love blessed Lauren and me. Time apart evaporated into hugs and tears of joy. My coworkers and I shared a common goal of educating students to the best of our ability, but we also cared about each other. This day was the personification of that love and community.

After a delicious buffet, Lauren was showered with beautiful, meaningful gifts and invaluable, yet sometimes funny, marriage wisdom. As gifts were passed around the circle of guests, for "oohs" and "ahhs," my smile fought to hide nausea and dizziness. Today required Academy Award-winning acting. I lost the battle to sit still, twisting and turning in pain. Excusing myself to the restroom meant parading my emaciated body before everyone, so I grounded myself on the loveseat, refusing to move. Heat rose inside me as the accompanying sweat began accumulating on my face. Lauren was enjoying her shower, but I needed it to end. I had little fight left in me for that day.

What I didn't know was that my friends were also hiding their concern for my gaunt appearance and weakness behind their smiles. As the shower ended, my dearest friend, Connie, pulled me aside, holding both of my hands with tears in her eyes. "Pam, everyone is worried about your health. What is your doctor saying?"

Jokingly, I offered her my best excuse. "Girl. You know me. I'm doing my typical overachieving thing, which translates to overdoing it. I'll be fine."

Connie's hug lingered with her plea. "Please get yourself checked out. Listen to me. Listen to Ralph. Please, Pam. Promise me."

Suddenly her hug grew into a prayer seeping into every pore of my body. Connie became the epitome of *Galatians 6:2 (NIV) as it states:*

"Carry each other's burdens, and in this way you will fulfill the law of Christ."

God was using those closest to me to get through to me. Their mirrors reflected my reality, unwanted or not. The added layer of exhaustion from fighting acceptance of my condition was too much for me. I needed God more than I'd ever needed Him before. What was wrong with me?

10
Surrender

Barely a week after the shower, I woke up expecting a normal March morning. Mom enjoyed her routine breakfast of oatmeal and toast as she watched me gingerly wall surf into the kitchen. I attempted to hold myself upright as I felt her evaluating my strength. I failed. Supporting myself against the counter, fidgeting with my robe belt helped tether me to reality. I fought to focus on Mom's words, as the bones in my legs softened to spaghetti and beads of sweat covered my forehead. A dark veil descended like a blackout curtain being drawn as her words faded away. In my desperate but futile attempt at steadying myself, I wanted to cry out in prayer, but I couldn't. It's in those moments that we can be assured of His promise in *Psalm 139:4 (NIV)*. He listens to the unspoken whispers of our hearts.

"Before a word is on my tongue, You, Lord, know it completely."

Mom's trembling voice faintly echoed in the blur of the moment. "Ralph! Ralph!"

Transitioning from the reality of my body about to meet the tiled floor, to sudden softness was a conundrum of confusion and comfort. What was happening to me? Warm hands stroked my face until I was able to semi-focus on Ralph's face staring back at me. Two of the biggest things in my life had collided and now swirled out of control: our daughter's wedding plans and my health threat. Mom and I used to remind each other of God's sovereignty in times like these.

"You ain't runnin' nothin'," we'd told each other with grateful laughter.

In the bedroom, Ralph worked to dress me. My precious mom's face reflected her concern as she stood frozen in our doorway. Known for her strength in adversity, now her worst fears were being realized right before her eyes. I was unable to offer any words of encouragement as Ralph slipped on my shoes. He wasted no time getting me into the car and heading to the hospital. However, the fifteen-minute ride felt like a cross-country trip.

Later, Mom told me that when Ralph and I left, she went straight to her room, fell on her knees, and cried out to God on my behalf. That is who she was in that moment, but also throughout her life: a fierce prayer warrior. I joked many times about buying her kneepads to extend her prayer time.

At the ER entrance, Ralph hurried inside to get a wheelchair and eased me into the intake area. Once we answered the routine questions, all we could do was wait. I leaned my head on his shoulder, slipped my hand into his, and closed my eyes. Why was I so exhausted?

The disinfectant stung my nostrils, and the cries of babies and the rush of frantic patients through the double doors helped keep me alert. To steady myself, I focused on the people around us and the stories they might carry.

"Why are they here?"

"What's their relationship to the person with them?"

"Is this their first ER visit, or are they frequent flyers?"

In stories God had written before I knew Him, none of these questions mattered, but in those moments, they were my tethers to reality.

After a wait that allowed me too much time to contemplate my condition, I settled into an emergency bed, where a nurse took my vitals and asked me the same questions Mom answered at her neurology appointments. My answers to these mental status inquiries were vague or nonexistent. A red flag should have been waving vigorously over my head as a sign of how they would proceed.

Meanwhile, if my room had a door, rather than a curtain, it would have been the revolving kind. Doctors, nurses, and lab techs were in and out like the carved figures on a merry-go-round. Throughout the endless tests, Ralph stood by my side or sat in the room's institutional-grade plastic chair, wrestling with it for comfort. My mind ran the gamut of possibilities as we waited. Lying there, confused and worried, Grandmother Sadie's words resurfaced as deep-rooted faith and hope.

"He wants to walk with you through life. He loves you," she said.

Her words inspired the courage I needed to trust the Lord deeper in a moment of weakness.

I prayed with confidence. "Lord Jesus, help me, please."

An ER doctor entered the room. He must have read my closed eyes as sleep, because he spoke to Ralph, not me. I lay there listening, refusing to expose my consciousness. The doctor explained they were admitting me and I'd be moved as soon as a regular room was available. He also apologized to Ralph because my test results had not been confirmed, explaining that they needed to consider every possibility.

If this was a time warp, I wanted out of it, and I expected answers. How did this happen to me? How would it end? All we knew was that I would not be going home tonight. My gut told me that things were about to get more serious.

11

Disobedience and Shock

The hours stretched endlessly, each tick of the clock louder than the last as daylight faded into quiet stillness. We sat in prayerful silence until Ralph mentioned informing our children about my situation. The potential seriousness of my case outweighed our concern for alarming them, so he called them.

"Your mom fell out at the house this morning. We're in the ER waiting for a regular room."

I heard the panic in their voices. "Wait. What's wrong with Mom? What do you mean she fell out?"

No matter how hard Ralph tried to convince Lauren to stay home until we had more answers, she was not having it. Stubbornness prompted her to toss some clothes in a bag and get on the road.

The number of times that I've surrendered my burdens at the Lord's feet to then snatch them back was embarrassingly high. Yet here I was racking my brain for my own solutions, yet again. A doctor interrupted my mental search, explaining that they wouldn't have my test results until the morning.

With my heart racing and palms sweating, I once again laid

my desperate plea before the Lord. All I could do was pray and hold onto a faith bigger than my fear as I waited.

In what I perceived to be no time, Lauren walked into my room. She must have driven with what her grandaddy called a lead foot. A piece of my heart relaxed a bit as Lauren and I embraced, holding on as long as we needed. When we released each other, I said, "Honey, you didn't have to come." I swiped tears from my eyes.

"How did you expect Ryan and me to react? Of course, we wanted to get here as soon as possible."

Laughing, even for a moment, renewed my spirit. If Lauren did nothing else while she was here, she infused joy into an otherwise somber hospital room. We all laughed as she recounted her negotiations with her brother that led to her sitting on the side of my bed. She explained that they both wanted to come right away, but she was freer to walk away from her job, so she won the debate.

Ryan is an empathic, driven person. He has a soft heart, but an intense drive to succeed. All his life, he's worked to emulate Ralph's strength and leadership qualities. On the other hand, he also prioritizes care and concern for me. Ryan's the tough guy with a soft heart for his mom. He checks on me almost every day. He's a caring son. He and Lauren have a supportive relationship, so he trusted her updates on my health.

Once Lauren understood my medical status and saw that I wasn't miserable, she went to our house to check on Mom. Knowing that Mom wasn't alone in her stress was comforting for Ralph and me. Lauren's human disobedience was obedience to God's plan.

Ralph and I fought individual battles against the incessant clock ticks and vitals checks in our desperate attempt to rest, to no avail. Twisting and turning in the hospital bed was no better defense than Ralph's fidgety posture on his plastic chair. Unspoken concern cloaked our little corner of the emergency room like thick fog. My internal pep talk assured me that I'd have some answers to this unbelievable dilemma by the time I was assigned a regular room. These high expectations didn't match the information we'd received so far, but hope was all I had.

Queasiness, confusion, and jaundice jockeyed for number one on my symptoms' top hits list. With looming fasting tests on the horizon, I was restricted to a liquid diet. Honestly, the mere thought of food created a storm in my stomach, so being restricted to sipping water was a blessing in disguise. My frustration grew when even my love of reading, my biggest passion, couldn't help me escape. Trying to focus on an overhandled hospital magazine brought on heightened anxiety and impatience. I struggled to anchor myself, repeating God's promise in Isaiah:

"But they who wait for the Lord shall renew their strength; they shall mount up with wings like eagles; they shall run and not be weary; they shall walk and not faint." Isaiah 40:31 (NIV)

PART FIVE
Walking in Faith

"Even though I walk through the darkest valley,
I will fear no evil, for you are with me..."
Psalm 23:4 (NIV)

12

Road Tripping

"There's nothing we can do for you here."

Seven words that cracked my world open.

One moment, I had been excited to tackle a long list of projects and phone calls. In the next moment, Dr. Willis's statement left me breathless, forcing me to face a reality I wasn't prepared for. With my signature scribbled on his tablet, arrangements were made to transport me to Butler Hospital in Fort Worth, Texas.

While I tried to steady myself, Ralph called Ryan, who promised to meet us in there, then updated Lauren and Mom at our house. Even though Mom was fairly self-sufficient, none of us were comfortable leaving her alone for an extended time. She was in her eighties, managing her own health challenges, all while worrying about mine.

Before I knew it, they formed a plan. Lauren would help Mom pack and drive her back to Dallas once the storm passed, staying with her as needed. I had to release that situation into God's hands. My energy was restricted to stretching in one direction, and right now every ounce of focus had to be on what lay ahead.

THERE'S NOTHING WE CAN DO FOR YOU HERE.

Sobering words for even the strongest Christian. With my soul gutted and wide open before God, my attempts at pretending were exposed. These defining moments in my life begged the question: Would I trust the Lord the way I told people I did? Was this a test of my faith, and would I pass? As Christians, we know the way to salvation is through believing in Jesus Christ. We must also acknowledge the charge God gives us to be obedient and measure our faith and actions against His Word. It was my time to live what I'd believed through trials that paled compared to this one.

I thought back on my parents' pivotal decision to raise me to love and trust God. They made sure that we attended church services, Sunday School, and special programs that the church celebrated. They set a Christian example at home by teaching me to pray beyond meal blessings and to read my Bible. I understood that my relationship with God was my own to be cultivated or ignored. There were times when I tended those seeds of faith that my parents planted. There were also times when the seeds lay dormant in God's hands waiting for my heart to return.

I thank so many strong Christian influences in my life for pouring into my faith bank at times that I had no appreciation for my need to increase my faith account.

If our faith accounts were as easy to monitor as our bank accounts. Instead of operating in the red, we could respect the overdraft notices and make new deposits of faith. Unfortunately, many Christians keep swiping their cards until the consequences negatively affect their lives. God monitors our faith accounts and sends us notices. He gives us free will to act on them or live with the consequences.

I reflected on conversations that I had with dear disciples that helped to encourage me to increase the balance in my account for such a time as this. The words of Reverend Williams' first wife stirred in my spirit without warning. One morning after church, in my preteen years, she approached me in the parking lot with this life-changing advice.

"You're going to need God as you live your life. Get to know Him for yourself now. He'll be there when you need Him."

No truer words have ever been spoken to me. Although my parents and Sunday School teachers had dedicated themselves to teaching and guiding me to this revelation, that parking lot encounter was pivotal in my spiritual beliefs. God used the pastor's wife to course-correct my heart directly toward Him and leave an indelible mark forever.

From then until this day's diagnosis, I can say that I haven't always vigorously pursued Him, but He has never left me. I put Him on a shelf and pulled Him down "as needed" for many years. Through maturity and life experiences, God allowed for my growth, drew me closer, and sparked a fire in me for a deeper relationship with Him.

As my mind refocused on the happenings around me, I was thankful that both of our adult children had loving partners who were willing to keep things going in their homes and to support them as needed. Caitlin and Quentin were working, praying, and waiting for updates. My family had a plan in place, and so did I. My plan was simple, yet the absolute best one. Trust God.

By this time, being awake most of the previous night caught up with me. When Ralph recognized my drowsiness, he took this opportunity to make a quick trip home to pack a bag for our upcoming trip. Between brief naps, I spent my time alone doing some serious thinking and praying.

"Why me, Lord? I know Your word says You never give us more than we can handle, but You have far more faith in me than I have in myself, as Your child. Show me my strength, because right now it's hidden behind my fear. It feels like my life is being stripped away at warp speed, Lord. Will this be the end for me? You've seen my human weaknesses. I've tried so hard to be faithful and strong. Keep me focused on You and Your plan. I trust that there is a bigger reason for what I'm going through. When it is revealed in Your timing, I will give You all the glory and praise. Stand with my family and strengthen them where they are weak. Give them hope and peace that only You can provide. Thank You, Lord. In Your son Jesus' name, Amen." Unable to stop the tears, I surrendered to them and to God's power.

Between other naps, God led me to scriptures in my Bible app. Psalms were my refuge and strength in those moments. I found power in this scripture:

"I have set the Lord always before me: because He is at my right hand I shall not be moved." Psalm 16:8 (KJV)

The words "I shall not be moved" drew me into the

comfort of Grandmother Sadie's modest church. My five-year-old self sat, wedged between cousins, watching Grandmother sing her faith and promise to the Lord. There she was, surrounded by the other church mothers, all seated on the pew reserved for them. "I shall not. I shall not be moved. Like a tree planted by the water, I shall not be moved." If the words of that African American spiritual provided peace for Grandmother, I would cling to them as well.

Even though Ralph wasn't gone long, time dragged. "Any word on transport yet?" he asked as he entered my room.

I shook my head, unable to hide my frustration. Ralph knew this pattern. When I was overwhelmed, I shut down. Dr. Willis had stressed how urgently I needed more advanced care, so every passing minute was a minute we didn't have to spare. The wall clock ticked in steady agreement with our rising anxiety. At last, the transport coordinator reappeared with Plan B.

"There's been a change. You'll go by ambulance instead of a helicopter. Storms have grounded all air transport. The crew is getting ready now, so it won't be much longer."

This unexpected setback threatened to raise our anxiety levels, but God...My heart rate and breathing settled down as soon as my God began a slide show of His past blessings and protection in my life.

Looking toward Ralph, she continued, "You aren't allowed to ride with your wife, but you're welcome to follow."

At this point, I had to cling to the comforting thought that Raph would be right behind the ambulance. Without another word, she left, and we processed. Plan B. Bottom line: At least there was a plan, and action items were being checked off the list.

My sole ambulance experience was as a teacher accompanying a student to the hospital. That was stressful enough for me. I dreaded the upcoming ride through the storm, but there was no other option. Fortunately, there was little time to be concerned. Within minutes, I was prepped for transport, including getting a much-appreciated sedative. With a second for a quick kiss goodbye, Ralph headed to his truck while my gurney rolled toward the ambulance bay and my future.

"Lord, let the doctors at this new hospital be the help that I need so badly. Your plan is my strongest hope." I prayed as silent tears spilled down my cheeks.

Even with the driver and paramedic onboard, loneliness pressed to the surface of my mind. I wanted Ralph. God took my hand and reminded me that I wasn't alone as I cried out to Him.

The sedative did little to calm my nerves. The turbulent ride refocused me on my immediate situation for the next two and one-half hours. Raging winds tossed us around like a cat playing with a toy mouse. The seatbelt strained to keep me tethered to the gurney with every bump along the highway. While assuring me they'd driven in worse storms, the paramedic seated beside me used his knees to help secure the gurney. With my eyes tightly closed to block out the lightning, my hands gripped the gurney's rail as if my life depended on it, because in that moment, it did. After an arduous trip, we arrived, and I prayed the physicians here could offer me more hope.

Entering Butler Hospital was like being dropped into an episode of The Twilight Zone. This early-sixties television series was based on an imaginary place beyond the realm of imagination. Combining the rocky ambulance ride with the complete absurdity of my unexpected diagnosis, and Dr. Willis' shocking pronouncement made this a Twilight Zone flashback for this Baby Boomer.

This facility was a beast compared to our local hospital. Unlike the night before, this hospital was ready. Staff met me at the door with my records in hand. I was poked and prodded from the instant the orderlies transferred me to my bed. The constant attention was comforting yet simultaneously concerning. I understood that I was getting this level of care due to the severity of Dr. Willis' diagnosis in Abilene. Still, the attention of qualified specialists sought by people worldwide was a spark of hope that recharged my faith. The Holy Spirit assured me that this was part of God's plan. With God as my anchor, I committed to His plan, in whatever form it took. Don't get me wrong. I was in no hurry to die and miss major family milestones. I prayed for time to experience any future grandchildren God may have had in His plan.

As the family's self-appointed empathetic fixer, planner, and people-pleaser, I executed my role seriously. This often meant overdoing things and pushing myself past my level of productivity without pain. My motto: Why give one hundred percent when two hundred is better?

Admittedly, this is an ongoing topic during my therapy sessions. I am a work in progress who needs a daily dose of grace. I couldn't help but wonder if I was learning a lesson the hard way.

Fibromyalgia is a hard teacher equipped with tough, unavoidable lessons, of which I was not prepared. It is also a thief. None of its treasures can be returned. It steals your current life and forces you into an unsolicited reality. It robbed me of my family role. It took away my ability to give everyone my all. Everything changed in the proverbial flip of a switch. Every part of my old self was altered or ripped from me. My ability to focus on reading and writing diminished. Working out, family and friend activities, and my confidence in my own body were all torn from my grasp. Now, my liver was failing me.

"What in the world, Lord?"

Ryan entered my room. I was excited to see him, but exhaustion and weakness disguised my enthusiasm. Hugging him pulled memories from my heart. They played in my mind like a family video, giving me a tiny glimpse of the beautiful life we shared. Assuring him I wasn't in pain seemed to relax his facial muscles, but he noticed my jaundiced coloring and frail body. I barely took up space under the sheets. My weight loss was noticeable.

Every doctor and nurse who entered checked my lucidity.

"Yes. I know what year it is, and I think I know who the president is. Oops.

Maybe not. I do know where I am and why I'm here... KIND OF... How about a few clues, Lord?"

Besides the confusion that accompanies liver failure, jaundice had me lit up like a jack-o-lantern. My yellow eyes and skin garnered interesting reactions from everyone the first time they saw me. With assurance that the jaundice would subside if my liver test numbers reversed, I lay there glowing and waiting.

In record time, test results showed that my liver was indeed failing. The interrogation intensified.

"What medications and supplements do you take? Are you in pain? What do you eat on a typical day? How much weight have you lost? When did you notice your first symptoms?" And on and on, day after day.

I'd become a human pincushion; hardly an hour passed without another blood draw or medication injection. The liver team, headed by Dr. Ash, did their due diligence. With little complaint from me, I trusted God had sent this accomplished hepatologist to walk this journey with me, and that was good enough for me. Dr. Ash was my Barnabas, as referenced below:

While they were worshipping the Lord and fasting, the Holy Spirit said, "Set apart for me Barnabas and Saul for the work to which I have called them." So, after they fasted and prayed, they placed their hands on them and sent them off." Acts 13:2-3 (NIV)

I had faith, but I also had physical limitations. Even with my best efforts at clinging to my faith, my body told a different story than the one in my tight grip. My appetite lessened by the day, and pounds fell off like dried leaves after the first frost. The smell of food caused my stomach to do somersaults and threaten to reverse gears. I didn't need to be a doctor to understand that I was not thriving. Fear camped out along with frustration. My stomach continued its rebellion. Ralph and others pleaded and even bribed me to eat, but I was not taking their bait. Like a toddler avoiding dreaded vegetables, I managed to prolong mealtime with negotiations and—as Grandmother Sadie called them—little hissy fits.

Then, Ryan unknowingly provided a nutrition option I could tolerate. As he casually sipped a smoothie while entering my room, I became intrigued. I considered whether it would sit well in my stomach. Noticing me staring, he offered me a taste, and I was hooked. No nausea, plus cool refreshment and nutrients, equaled daily smoothie runs. My nutrition woes were temporarily solved. I cried, "Thank you, Jesus! Yet again, You worked out an issue in my life."

Lying in bed for ten arduous days of testing and multiple daily exams, I prayed and fought for my life. My bilirubin, ALT, and AST liver enzymes were far from the normal range. They fluctuated slightly, but never enough to be normal and safe. These terms were foreign to me before a liver failure diagnosis upended my world. In fact, I knew very little about the liver's function. Unfortunately, Ralph and I were both becoming proficient in "liver speak."

Days turned into weeks, while my daily routine remained the same. *Philippians 4:6-7* became my anchor scripture. It encouraged me to keep praying and trusting God to walk with me. I prayed for a stronger dose of the peace this scripture promised as I read or recited it:

"Do not be anxious about anything, but in everything by prayer and supplication with thanksgiving let your requests be made known to God. And the peace of God, which surpasses all

understanding, will guard your hearts and your minds in Christ Jesus." Philippians 4:6-7 (NIV)

Dr. Ash and his team studied every prescription drug in my jumbo bag and continued to be baffled for days. In the end, they unearthed the culprit. The muscle relaxer that I started taking about a month before my decline had caused my liver to fail. To lessen the blow of the amazing odds, Dr. Ash jokingly told me I should buy a lottery ticket because very few people beat thirty-thousand-to-one odds of anything. Those were the odds of the muscle relaxer causing liver damage. Somehow, lucky was the absolute last thing I felt in this moment, but I was grateful they'd found the source of the problem.

13

Reality Shifts

The events of the last thirty-six hours shoved Lauren into a role she never asked for but had no choice but to claim. Responsibility settled on her shoulders fast and heavy, and if there was one thing Lauren had always possessed, it was grit.

Before her father's call about my emergency room visit, her world revolved around work and wedding plans. She, Rae, and I functioned like a seamless trio, moving every detail forward with purpose. Then I was ripped out of the equation. In an instant, Lauren had to assume my share as well as caregiver for her "granny."

Like a grenade, Lauren lies dormant until someone pulls her fuse. Then, at "go time," she fires up and gets things done with authority. This was certainly one of those times. With Lauren's help, Mom settled back into her house in Dallas. She was content to stay home and pray rather than sit in a hospital waiting room. When Lauren called my aunt to explain our situation, she gladly agreed to spend some time with Mom to free up Lauren. Not everyone is blessed with an extended family that shows up in times of need, but God can soften hearts and change situations. I encourage everyone to reach out to their loved ones and even acquaintances without anticipating a negative response. This scripture bears instruction for loved ones, and I can testify that my God has supernatural powers beyond our comprehension. Trust Him without question, for your needs. He will meet you in your faith and help you forgive and love as he describes in these scriptures:

"Above all, love each other deeply, because love covers a multitude of sins." 1 Peter 4:8 (NIV)

"Bear with each other and forgive one another if any of you has a grievance against someone, forgive as the Lord forgives you." Colossians 3:13 (NIV)

Without a doubt in my mind, I can picture Mom storming the throne of God on my behalf. Our bond was more than that of a mother and a daughter, but also one of best friends. Her faith was the quality that I admired most about her. She was my "on her knees" prayer warrior in every aspect of my life and those of our family. Her intercessory prayers had seen us through infinite trials, some of which were battles won behind the veil, but Mom was fervent and convinced Jesus can do what He says He can do in this scripture:

James 5:16 tells us that "The effectual fervent prayer of a righteous man availeth much. (KJV)

As my eyes met Lauren's, my heart swelled. We had the same strong connection that Mom and I shared, which was something I always prayed for. However, my deepest thoughts of compassion were blocked by sadness. I could only whisper them within my soul.

"It saddens me that Lauren is now tasked with handling so

many of the wedding plans when she should be enjoying every minute of this memorable time."

Even though my heart was with Lauren, I had no choice but to focus on my health. Tears pooled in Lauren's eyes. She hugged me, we soaked each other in for as long as we both needed. Her hug was reassuring, yet it pained me at the same time. I had no doubt that Lauren and Rae would handle everything for the wedding. Instead of drowning in her sea of concerns about my recovery, nothing would stop her from filling my shoes to get the job done.

Organizing using binders has been my thing since high school. Some people function in chaos. I thrive in organization. Give me a project and watch me set up a color-coded, tabbed binder in a split second. Lauren knew my binder was my wedding bible and my constant companion since proposal day. It would help her pick up where I'd left off when my world was turned upside down by liver failure.

"Where's your wedding binder, Mom? I need your notes."

"Dad had no idea we'd need it at the hospital. He'll go back soon and bring it. In the meantime, update Rae on my situation. Thankfully, she has most of my notes on her laptop."

After a brief conversation, my eyelids began to close like blackout curtains slowly being drawn shut. Thoughts of my hospital experience and wedding planning swirled together just as my favorite smoothie ingredients do in a blender. With a quick kiss on my forehead and an "I love you, Mom," as her parting gift, Lauren walked into her assignment, committed to being strong for me.

As Ryan took calls and answered emails, I drifted in and out of sleep. Being together was comforting for both of us.

Other days, I woke from naps to find my beloved sister, Tameko, smiling at me. She was a source of joy and a ray of sunshine. Every visit comforted me like a frightened child hugging a teddy bear. She could read me well enough to know when to be a quiet presence in the room as I silently wrestled with my thoughts, or when to remind me of some of our crazy antics so we could share a much-needed belly laugh.

I spent my childhood asking my parents and God for a sister. In my mind, this meant a young playmate and a forever friend. My parents made it clear that there would be no more babies in our family. As I got older, it meant a confidante and fellow mischief-maker. But the man upstairs had a plan.

God blessed our whole family when He brought Tameko into our lives. Even though she had a loving family of her own, Dad and Mom began mentoring Tameko. As time went on, their student mentoring evolved into a deeper, supportive relationship. As she spent more time with them, she and I developed a beautiful relationship as well. Her heart was torn between her biological family and the new family she'd found in us. Tameko was embraced by our huge extended family. Not only was she welcome, but family members and strangers were constantly amazed by our resemblance. They automatically assumed that we were biological sisters.

Pride filled me when I introduced her as my bonus sister. My childhood prayers were answered in God's way and in His timing. He gave me Tameko. We began walking alongside each other through whatever life threw at us. Growing closer with every late-night phone call, shared tearful crisis, family gathering, and more, our bond strengthened. Throughout our adult lives, we each matured and set off on our own paths, but our hearts were drawn back to each other.

Tameko walked every step of my health journey with me. Her level of commitment and love was an unmatched gift and sacrifice. I could trust her to be my sister, confidante, gatekeeper of my room, and so much more. She was the rock star of protecting my privacy when visitors, no matter how well-meaning, made it difficult for me to rest.

Quentin visited as time allowed, while juggling work, a stressed fiancé, and a long list of wedding to-dos. His smile was always a refreshing blessing in my day.

Our daughter-in-love, Caitlin, assumed the exact role that I hoped she would. Keeping Ryan's faith energized was exactly what I prayed she would do. I knew Caitlin had strong faith, but I'd never witnessed it in crisis. Ryan later shared with me how much of a prayer warrior she was during my crisis. With prayer as her first response, rather than her last resort, she unknowingly joined Mom as an intercessor for me. I'm forever grateful.

Tough times either make or break us as individuals and as families. In our case, they united us in purpose and faith. I understand that family dynamics differ, especially in moments of crisis. We have moments of selfishness and little faith, just like any other family. If you're struggling with family support, I remind you that despite your family situation, you are not alone. You have a Heavenly Father who's always with you, with outstretched hands.

The reality outside my room was that the wedding day window was rapidly closing. Ryan and Tameko freed up Ralph and Lauren to check off more to-dos. Running on fumes, Ralph made multiple day trips home and back to deliver wedding décor. Watching him functioning as a determined ball of nerves heightened my concern for his health as much as my own. I knew my husband too well to believe his assurances that he was fine. My response and my hope were in prayer.

In my better moments, I pleaded with Lauren for wedding details. Helping with this wedding, as well as Ryan and Caitlin's, was the most important project in my life, besides our own wedding. The sadness and guilt of missing out on the total experience burrowed its way into my psyche and hounded me daily, but this was my new reality. My greatest contribution in this season was simply to fight for my health.

PART SIX
Walking a New Path

"This is what the Lord says: 'Stand at the crossroads and look; ask for the ancient paths, ask where the good way is, and walk in it, and you will find rest for your souls.'"
Jeremiah 6:16 (NI

14

The "T" Word

With the new test results revealing my liver numbers trending negatively, Dr. Ash pulled Ralph into the hallway for an urgent conversation. I needed a liver transplant as soon as possible.

"If your wife doesn't get a new liver soon, you won't be taking her home alive."

Later, Ralph shared with me that hearing those words hit him like a Muhammad Ali one-two punch. They forced him to anchor his soul in God deeper than ever before. He resolved to hold this information until the doctor shared it with me. Dr. Ash was preparing Ralph to be strong for me.

During my second week at Butler Hospital, Dr. Ash walked in, and his eyes centered directly on Ralph. In that moment, their wordless communication spoke volumes. With my eyes laser-focused on my doctor, I reached for Ralph's hand as he drew near. It was time for "the conversation" I had not been privy to before now.

With no hesitation and direct delivery, Dr. Ash began.

"Mrs. Porter, your liver numbers continue to trend negatively. At this point, a transplant is your only hope. Do you understand what I'm telling you?"

My nod was the only recognition I could muster. He continued.

"My team has a plan ready to implement. With your permission, we will order the necessary testing required before presenting your case to our hospital transplant board. If you pass all the tests, the board will consider the urgency of your case, your overall health, and your potential as a liver recipient. They will decide whether to submit your name to UNOS (United Network for Organ Sharing)." He paused for a few seconds. "Are you still with me, Mrs. Porter?"

This time, I nodded more firmly. Although overwhelmed by this information, I needed him to understand that I was ready to fight for my life.

"Yes, I'm with you all the way, Doc."

"Okay, then, you stay strong, and my team will get to work on our plan. Your job is to lie there and rest. We'll do the rest."

With a tentative smile, I replied, "Good, because right now, that's about all I can do."

Dr. Ash's pat on my shoulder was evidence of his support and a glimmer of hope in the darkness. I silently thanked God for him as he left my room. Though Dr. Ash's update stirred more concern, I recognized God's hand all over this storm.

"*Lord, the words, 'only hope,' take me back to Abilene, where I heard, 'There is nothing we can do for you,'*" I cried in my soul. "Only hope" sounds dangerously close to the same prognosis. *"Let this transplant work, Lord, if it is your will. I'm hanging on, but you see my struggle. I've tried so hard to honor you with how I live. I do my best to be Your light for others to see. But now, you're taking me through the hardest trial of my life. I know we should never ask why, but I also know that you can read it on my heart: "Why me? Why now? Make it make sense. Now would be good, but if not, I'll keep holding on until your plan for me is made evident. You are my everlasting hope. In Jesus' name, Amen."*

Ralph pulled me into a bear hug. "We've got this, babe, because God's got us. You're going to be just fine."

Those words of affirmation and comfort were the balm that I craved so deeply. They were enough to refocus me and support my prayer. I could trust the visible evidence of my condition or the invisible, omnipotent power of my savior. As I wrestled with this new information, my soul cried out in assurance. The Holy Spirit gave me two scriptures that solidified the muddled thoughts:

"Who has believed our message and to whom has the arm of the Lord been revealed?" Isaiah 53:1 (NIV)

"And now, O Lord, for what do I wait?" My hope is in You." Psalm 39:7

With God's word as confirmation, I silently recommitted my faith in the Lord and reaffirmed my choice to believe His promises in that moment, just as I had throughout my life, with Him as my faithful companion. A transplant offered hope, but my true hope was anchored in the promise of being a child of God.

A series of tests was completed at a rapid pace. On some occasions, multiple technicians, each with their own specialized equipment, were lined up in a queue. Every test except the bone marrow biopsy was completed at my bedside. Otherwise, I lay in wait as the technician parade proceeded in and out of my room.

The next day, as Dr. Ash entered the room, the first thing I noticed was the rare smile on his face.

"Mrs. Porter, all your test results were negative. You have no other medical concerns other than fibromyalgia. I will present your case to the hospital transplant board tomorrow.

With that green light, we waited prayerfully for the board's decision. The next day, Dr. Ash appeared with yet another of his encouraging smiles.

"I have wonderful news. The board approved your case, so your name has been submitted to UNOS as a high-priority case. Now we wait for your new liver and do our best to keep you comfortable. Do you have any questions?"

"I feel relieved and afraid at the same time. Please just tell us what we need to know."

Dr. Ash anticipated my naivete about transplants, so he went on to explain the process.

"When a donor liver becomes available, surgery preparation will shift into high gear. My team and I will perform your transplant. You will remain here in the intensive care unit for several days of strict monitoring. If there are no complications, you'll be downgraded to a regular room for another two or three weeks before being discharged. During this time, you'll receive more counseling and post-transplant instructions. Does this all make sense?"

Even though the fact that we were seriously discussing

transplant procedures was surreal, Dr. Ash's explanation made perfect sense. I just didn't want to be the one in this situation.

"Again, Lord, make it make sense."

"Yes," I answered. It makes sense, but what if there are no donors anytime soon?"

"If your liver markers worsen dramatically, I will encourage you to solicit family members and friends to get tested as possible live donors. The matching donor would donate a portion of their liver. Over time, that portion would regrow, and they shouldn't have any long-term complications. For now, though, let's focus on option one."

Ralph and I agreed that the live donor option was overwhelming, but, if necessary, we would have no other choice. Until then, we were Team Option One.

"You and Mr. Porter are scheduled for the earliest pre-transplant counseling session. We need to get you both prepared for when a liver becomes available."

After a few other details, Dr. Ash left us with much to contemplate. What would counseling be like? Was there a lot to know before the transplant? We wouldn't have long to wait for these answers.

In the meantime, we understood that this was the doctor's best plan. God's hand led us to this specific hospital and team of doctors. We trusted their expert opinions, BUT GOD

15

Option One

Early the next morning, a friendly gray-haired woman in her sixties entered my room. She shook my hand, opened her laptop, and handed us a folder.

"I'm Joyce, your transplant coordinator. I'm here to help you navigate this process as painlessly as possible."

Ralph and I exchanged a breath, bracing for what was ahead. I thought I should take notes, but Joyce assured me, "Everything we cover today will be in your folder, so you can just listen."

The extent of our transplant knowledge was about remaining on anti-rejection drugs, as well as the importance of attending all follow-up appointments. Joyce covered those points before explaining the importance of a strong support group. Having people around me for moral support, as well as any physical assistance necessary, could make a significant difference in my recovery. We appreciated and understood these guidelines. There were other aspects of the process that neither of us had even considered.

"Do you have family in the area who would allow you to

live with them for six weeks to six months after your transplant?" Joyce asked matter-of-factly.

We were stunned.

"Six months living away from home with relatives?" Shocked, Ralph and I echoed each other.

Even though we had family members in the area who would graciously open their homes to us, we could not fathom imposing on them to that extent. Such a big ask wasn't one we were prepared to make unless there were no other options.

Joyce explained that living within proximity to the hospital and my doctor's office would be imperative to my recovery, as well as a requirement for the transplant. The follow-up appointments would initially be as frequently as twice weekly. They would lessen over time, but remaining close would still be necessary in case of emergency complications.

Reading our overwhelmed facial expressions, Joyce offered a second option. She told us we could live in a house similar to a Ronald McDonald house that provides post-transplant housing and support.

"Any questions?" she asked.

"Not right now. I think we both need some time to process everything. We'll probably have questions at some point, though," I answered.

The whole situation unfolded like a scene from a hospital drama, not my life. Plus, things were moving at warp speed. As a trained professional, Joyce seemed to recognize the weight of her information on us, so she excused herself.

As Ralph and I reflected on this new information, he reminded me that, as in other trials that had loomed heavily in our lives, our choice to continue walking with God was the strength and anchor that we needed. I did my best to make Him my number one priority. I don't want to come across as some "holier than thou" person who never experiences doubt, fear, or frustration with God.

Believe me. I struggled at times. Tears of doubt and fear flowed. Some of my prayers became more like arguments as I lay in the quiet of the midnight hour, as senior church mothers used to call it. I stormed God's throne for more than strength. I wanted an explanation for my circumstances. I needed assurance of its purpose in my life.

If we expect to be one hundred percent all in with God three hundred sixty-five days a year, we're setting ourselves up for disappointments and feelings of failure. God is a forgiving God and a faithful one as well.

In *Deuteronomy 31:6 (NIV),* Moses told the Israelites, *"Be strong and courageous. Do not be afraid or terrified because of them, for the Lord, your God, goes with you; He will never leave you nor forsake you."*

When we stray momentarily, or even longer, He's always there awaiting our return. I kept the word, "Thank you, Lord," in my spirit at all times.

Music, like walking, had always been therapeutic for me. I attribute that to the fact that my parents indulged my interest in music, even though neither of them was musically inclined. They bought me a piano, and I began lessons at age seven. Even though practicing scales and competing in music theory competitions weren't what I had in mind, I had to practice them. My music teacher was excellent, and she required both before learning to play my favorite songs.

Since those early lessons, I've appreciated the power of music to touch every aspect of our lives, from celebrations to tragedies. It has ministered to me and has been the soundtrack to life's highs and lows. The lyrics speak to my situation, and the melodies calm my soul. Give me a little "It Is Well with My Soul", "How Great Thou Art" or "Great Is Thy Faithfulness" and I feel transported to Heaven, walking the streets of gold. Music soothes me in times of crisis. We must all discover what ministers to us most effectively because every one of us will need comfort when trials come, as they certainly will.

PART SEVEN
Walking with Help

"And do not forget to do good and to share with others, for with such sacrifices God is pleased."
Hebrews 13:16 (NIV)

16

Sharing and Caring

When the children came to visit, Ralph took the lead in sharing my latest update. I was content and thankful to allow him to do the talking because verbalizing the word "transplant" was beyond my capacity at that moment.

"I'm glad you're both here because we have some news." Ralph began.

Doing his best to explain the doctor's plan as simply as possible, he finished with the kicker.

"Mom needs a transplant to live. They've placed her on the UNOS transplant list."

I added, "I know that God has a plan for me. He can turn this around. He can find me a donor if He chooses to do so. If He plans to take me home to heal me, then none of us can delay or stop His plan. We're choosing to continue walking with God, and we need you to do the same."

Before either of them could speak, I continued. "I'm not afraid of dying. My concern is for both of you. I'm praying for your strength and faith to carry you through whatever lies ahead. I love you so much. Just keep praying."

Lauren sliced into my words. "Mom, stop talking about dying! You are not going to die!"

Talking about dying can be extremely uncomfortable for some people. In fact, most people are afraid of death and afraid to discuss it.

My response to Lauren was straight from my heart. "I'm not giving up. It means that I am accepting God's Will, whatever that may be. At your ages, I don't expect you to have my same perspective. Just please trust God for my future."

Reading Ryan as I usually can, his deflected eyes and wringing hands revealed his attempt to draw inward. He needed time and space to process the "T" word.

Often, when God puts something heavy or difficult on my heart, I need time and space to wrestle with it. I am so thankful He knows that about me, and He gives me what I need, while fully aware of the outcome long before me. Both children's reactions were loving signs of concern that resonated deeply within me.

After that day, I reiterated my thoughts on death repeatedly to anyone who would listen. My acceptance increased my strength and hope in ways that even I didn't understand. This was between God and me. I did not need to fight for my life. He was fighting for me. As Yolanda Adams sings, "This Battle is the Lord's." What a relief to have a loving, powerful God in complete control, as opposed to my weak attempt at controlling things. Resting in His peace and power became my daily prayer and blessing.

Ralph updated everyone via his family and friends' text

thread. Some were shocked, not realizing the extent of my illness. Others, like our dear friend, Ron, had done their own research and understood the necessity of live donors when organs aren't readily available. Ralph hadn't cast a net for donors, but we received a message from Ron offering to be tested as a live donor. Such a selfless offer was difficult to wrap my head around. Together, Ralph and I struggled for adequate verbiage to thank Ron. We assured him that if the situation was warranted, we would accept his offer.

After our exchange, my mind went to this scripture about the body of Christ:

"...so that there should be no division in the body but that its parts should have equal concern for each other." 1 Corinthians 12:25 (NIV)

Each member of the body of Christ should have equal concern for all its members. Ron's text was a beautiful demonstration of unity and obedience that touched my heart deeply.

Even though Ralph had done a wonderful job of updating everyone, I am one of those people who need privacy, especially when I'm stressed or sick. Visitors drain my energy and cause more stress, even loved ones. The introvert in me, combined with my Fibro sensitivities, forced me to seek solitude whenever possible. Fibro triggers include stress, noise, crowds, fluorescent lights, and more. Most of the time, Ralph could read me well enough to steer the visits to a timely end without being rude. Other times, I fought hard to hide my body's reaction to these triggers, but some visits left me fighting tears.

My husband steadied himself for me, but beyond my room,

our children saw him unravel in ways that shocked them. For so many years and in so many ways, Ralph had been the fixer in our family. Now he faced something he could not fix. He was truly afraid.

I hoped his solo drives home helped him decompress, that he was using the time to talk to God. The lyrics of the song, "Just a Little Talk with Jesus," ran through my mind. They reminded me of the hope I felt every time I heard that song in my grandmother's church.

I have certainly called out to Him while driving alone, and He has met me in my car, just as powerfully as He has in moments of quiet prayer at home or on a church pew. He meets us wherever we are, literally and metaphorically.

Ralph refused multiple offers of help with getting the wedding décor items transported to Rae, but he chose to handle everything himself. That's the man I married. He's not perfect, nor am I. He is, however, a strong man of God and a loving husband, father, grandfather, and friend. We've endured trials and celebrated joys for over forty-five years of marriage. By the grace of God and our commitment to stick it out in the tough times, we have walked onward.

In the stillness and quiet of the night, Ralph often shared people's messages and prayers with me. Between the births of our children and a few surgeries for me, he had spent many nights at my bedside. Favorite TV shows and sports filled most of those nights. These moments, though, brought a deeper, more sacred weight. The seriousness of my condition warranted more appreciation of every minute that we were blessed to spend together. Admittedly, we had often taken our time together for granted, but not in this situation. God had our full attention. His words in Psalm 39 were a convicting reminder.

"O Lord, remind me how brief my time on earth will be. Remind me that my days are numbered—how fleeting my life is. You have made my life no longer." Psalm 39:4 (NIV)

Life beyond the sterile walls of my hospital room seemed to be on pause, but people were going about their lives. The wedding thundered toward us like a herd of wild horses. In desperation, I begged Dr. Ash to release me to attend the wedding, just long enough to witness the vows. In retrospect, I realize how absurd my request for a hospital day pass was. I would have gone by ambulance if they had made that stipulation. We've all heard the saying, "Desperate times call for desperate measures." I was there.

Of course, the doctors refused to entertain even one of my repeated irrational pleas. If a liver became available, I would have immediate transplant surgery. If one wasn't available soon, I would remain in the hospital for monitoring and begin the live donor search. Either way, the "ifs" won. I would not be attending the wedding.

Lauren had no time to allow her emotions to get the best of her. When Ralph brought my wedding binder back from Abilene, what she saw was shocking. My perfectly organized binder was an information explosion. Sticky notes full of names, addresses, and lists burst forth from every edge of the binder. This was not how I formerly functioned. My illness showed up in that book before I ever had a test to prove it.

One day while visiting, Lauren shocked me with the words, "Mom, we need to postpone the wedding."

Stunned by her pronouncement, every muscle in my body tensed while my heart and mind reacted in sadness and with grit simultaneously. I hurt for Lauren, and I knew it was time to man up. I was not going to allow my situation to sidetrack our daughter and future son-in-law's special day.

"God, hide my pain and guilt. Give me the words and the strength to encourage Lauren. May she feel my heart, but also my dogged determination through my words," I silently prayed.

"Absolutely not, sweet girl. You are walking down that aisle as a beautiful bride to your groom, as planned. This is just a hitch, not a date extension."

"We can get married after you're feeling better. We don't mind waiting because we want you at the wedding."

"No ma'am. Selfishly, I need this wedding to happen. Otherwise, my self-imposed guilt will eat me alive."

Knowing me to be as determined as her granny, Lauren reluctantly relented, promising that things would go on, even though she could not imagine getting married without me there.

Rae worked closely with Lauren and exceeded the expectations of any wedding planner. Juggling her substitute mom, planner, and therapist hats qualified her for the wedding planner extraordinaire award. Ralph and I are forever indebted to her.

As I lay in bed one morning, staring mindlessly at some random game show, Rae caught me completely off guard.

"What are you doing here? Don't you have more important things to do than visit the mother of the bride?" I jokingly asked.

After a long, heartfelt hug, she replied, "I promise not to stay long or tire you out, but right now, you are my priority."

The sole purpose of her visit broke me. I invited Rae to sit on the bed near me and began peppering her for wedding details.

"I'm not here to go over details, Pam. Trust me. I have everything under control. I came to assure you that your job is to focus on your health and not worry. I will do whatever it takes to make this wedding everything Quentin and Lauren envision. I will take care of your sweet girl. And if we need to roll you down that aisle in a wheelchair or even FaceTime the whole thing, you will not miss it," Rae promised.

By now, tears drenched the front of my gown as I managed to eke out a few words through sobs.

"Thank you for stepping up to fill the void that I know Lauren feels right now. I appreciate you more than you will ever comprehend."

Rae kept her visit short and to the point by ending it with one more hug. I can't imagine another planner would care for the mother of the bride to this extent. Yet again in my life, God provided the right person to walk alongside me before I had any idea just how much I would need her. He does some of His best work behind the veil of our daily lives. I would have given anything for even a glimpse of what was to come.

17
In the Details

Hospital life was a blur of lab draws, liver updates, and UNOS progress reports. My numbers fluctuated slightly, but not enough to indicate an upturn in my condition. My status remained the same: Critical Condition and in need of a transplant. My biggest battle continued to be getting food down. The sight and smell stirred waves of nausea at levels beyond my experience. Stubbornly, I continued pleading with Dr. Ash to allow me to attend the wedding. He, of course, refused every time. Who gets released in critical condition? I prayed I might be the first. Ultimately, I was forced to accept that FaceTime might be my only bridge to my loved ones, if I was still coherent by the big day.

Lauren pressed forward with Rae's guidance and support, checking off to-dos and adding more each day. I did my best to encourage her, noting the strained smile that accompanied her claim she was "fine." We'd shared talks about her dream of floating through her bridal journey with me by her side. Instead, her brave face hid pain and disappointment.

I was, however, grateful for Quentin's mother, Toni, Ryan, Caitlin, Tameko, Lauren's bridesmaids, and other family for standing in the gap for me. Their support was immeasurable. Running errands, finishing projects, hunting down necessary items, and so much more, with no hesitation, was literally priceless. Rae and this dream team kept the wedding train rolling down the track.

Despite my prognosis, everyone proceeded with the assumption that somehow, I would make it to the wedding. Tameko graciously volunteered to stay with me while Ralph and Mom went to Abilene to gather her clothes for the wedding, as well as mine. Thank God for Tameko's loving care and humor to help me relax and even laugh, reminiscing about some of our silly antics. In those moments, flashbacks to our late-night conversations were a welcome respite from my reality.

My phone rang, and it was Ralph and Mom on a FaceTime. I could see they were at our house.

"Hey, babe. We need help finding everything you bought to wear this weekend. Your mom and I have searched your closet, but we can't find some things your mom knows you planned to wear."

Even though I was groggy from an afternoon nap, I was excited. Their voices sounded like hope, which I desperately craved.

"Give the phone to Mom. I can help her find them," I said.

Poor Mom had FaceTimed once in her life, so she was understandably overwhelmed by the concept of seeing me in a

Fort Worth hospital speaking to her at our house in Abilene. We had a little laugh about that before I sent her on a scavenger hunt. A nurse came into my room in the middle of the video call. Even she was amused by our conversation. I did my best to direct Mom toward clothing options for the rehearsal dinner. While she kept digging, I bragged a little.

"I have the best mom and husband in the world. They're doing their best to get me ready for our daughter's wedding."

With a wink and a smile, the nurse left to allow me to finish the scavenger hunt. Mom held up item after item for my approval until we coordinated a western-themed outfit for the dinner. Blowing kisses to Mom and Ralph, we ended the call, and I wiped a tear of love and joy.

Before I realized it, Easter arrived. It was our first major holiday spent in a hospital. We traditionally gathered with immediate and extended family on holidays. This year was cloaked in faith, fear, hope, and change. No matter what, though, Jesus' resurrection would not pass without honor and praise.

On the other hand, my Fibro brain dreaded the day in advance. The barrage of well-meaning visitors, coupled with overstimulation issues and sensitivities, had me praying for a quiet, reflective day.

When Ralph went downstairs Easter morning to grab some breakfast, God met him with another plan. He noticed a flyer for Easter services scheduled at the hospital. One service was about to begin, so he texted me explaining that he was going to attend if I was okay by myself. I was rarely alone, so I encouraged him to attend the service.

Against all odds, I drifted into one of the best naps I'd had in weeks. Lulled by the monitor's beeps, I rested like I used to under the summer breezes of Grandmother's screened-in porch. I was awakened by Ralph's return. He shared that he had attended two services. Joy filled my heart knowing that he had the opportunity to spend time with God and worship Him.

Ralph asked me about my rest. The realization hit us that I had slept for over two hours. Hmmm. I wondered if sleeping longer was a sign of something good or bad. Before Ralph could help me freshen up and get dressed, Dr. Ash and his hepatology team filled the room—young and old, diverse, eager to learn. Watching them hang on his every word comforted me. Dr. Ash was internationally known as a liver specialist. God had clearly placed me in the right hands.

In anticipation of Dr. Ash's latest update, Ralph and I clasped hands. He stood a little straighter, and I adjusted myself in my bed to sit up taller and face whatever news was to come. Dr. Ash stepped closer to my bed, as did his team.

"We have your latest results and an update from UNOS."

For a split second, my heart skipped a beat, hoping that maybe UNOS had a liver for me. The sensation of Ralph squeezing my hand a little tighter was a reality check and reminder to focus.

"At this point, your liver numbers are fluctuating. Some are pushing the top of the safe range, while most of them are going up and down within the danger zone."

Ralph interjected, "How much danger are you talking about, doctor?" His eyes were on me, and so were Dr. Ash's.

"Mrs. Porter, your overall numbers are not promising. Your prognosis is grim. As of now, UNOS has not found an available liver match, but we will continue to monitor their responses. You will be updated as soon as we have news about a donor. Your mental health is vitally important, so for now, try to rest and remain positive."

Silence engulfed us as Dr. Ash left the room. Clutching Ralph's hand even tighter, tears of acceptance streamed down my cheeks to my pillow. Ralph's heartbeat pounded against my chest as we embraced. No words. Only love and faith. No Easter bunnies or egg hunts on our minds. This Easter Sunday's focus would be exactly where it should be, celebrating Jesus' resurrection and power on the cross and hope in Him, as it is written in Isaiah.

"But those who hope in the Lord will renew their strength; they shall mount up like eagles; they shall run and not be weary; they shall walk and not faint." Isaiah 40:31 (NIV)

Despite our focus, the well-meaning parade of visitors pierced the deafening silence of my room. With tears whisked away and strained smiles, we welcomed all who flooded my room. The parade continued as visitors stopped by after their Easter services ended. Between cat naps, I conjured up the strength to engage with family and friends, but the words "your prognosis is grim" had settled in my heart and stolen my joy.

Some visitors offered prayers, while others' hugs and hand-holding spoke for them. As the day wound down, so did my energy level. I was left with the visitors I always treasured in the room—my children. They were precious gifts and always welcome. Their smiles, funny stories, and hugs were like Santa at the end of the Christmas parade. I couldn't think of a better way to end my day than with their love. They will never appreciate how much their mere presence ministered to me that day.

Peaceful silence embraced the room after the children went home. Beeping monitors and announcements from the hospital's hallway speakers reset our minds back to just the two of us facing the battle that defined this season of our lives.

After appreciating the quiet for a few moments, Ralph and I enjoyed some reflection on our day. I shared with him how I had enjoyed the best nap I'd had since being admitted and possibly even before. Because of his vigilance and awareness of my stress level, I was able to handle the visitors with minimal sensory overload.

Ralph shared thoughts about the hospital's Easter services. Listening to him relive his experience comforted me more than he realized. I could hear spiritual renewal and peace in every one of his words. God had met Ralph when he needed it the most. He had refilled Ralph's cup to continue the fight. I thanked God silently for His goodness and grace toward my husband.

Please savor your quiet moments, no matter our circumstances. Those memories will remain precious beyond our current situation. Every day has the potential to be a good day if we face whatever it brings with an attitude of gratitude and peace, knowing that God is ultimately in control.

Two days came and went with little or no change, which

was a double-edged sword. No UNOS transplant news. No significant positive changes in my liver numbers. God was testing our faith in this valley. I know that God is our teacher in every aspect of life. Hearing people say that the teacher is quiet during the test always comforts me. None of us should feel abandoned in times of trial, but rather, we should see these times as opportunities to draw closer to Him. We should remember His past triumphs in our lives and His promises for our futures. Thanks to God's mercy, we are still here. He has never left us before. Why should He now? This kind of faith requires spiritual maturity. The more we know God's character, the more we can respect and honor His power. So maybe His silence in our test is twofold:

1. To allow us to show Him what we have learned from this and prior tests.

2. To encourage us to go deeper and learn more from our testing.

My desperate prayers, heartfelt praise, and worship were my response to God's silence in my circumstance. I wouldn't be honest unless I shared that on this journey toward spiritual maturity, I had moments of weakness. My prayers were sometimes cries of despair and anguish.

"Why me, Lord?" I often repeated. "I've tried so hard to be a good Christian, not just the world's idea of one, but a Christian with a real relationship with You. I feel closer to You now than at any time in my life. I trust You. I just don't understand why this is happening. Help me see You in the midst of my illness. Lord, I need so badly to hold onto the promise that You're working this out for my good."

The word "endurance" is a loaded word, whose weight is determined by our circumstances. I embraced endurance during this season of my life, accepting the weight along with the promise found in *Hebrews 10:36 (NIV).*

"You need to persevere so that when you have done the will of God, you will receive what He has promised."

Simeon and Anna faithfully endured, facing death from old age, to meet the Messiah. Their endurance was in active obedience, including fasting, praying, and seeking God's Word. Their obedience was worth every sacrifice when they met Jesus. I did my best to model my endurance on that of Simeon and Anna. I prayed, was honest with God, and did my best to shine His light through the darkness of my season. My endurance increased my faith exponentially. According to other family members, they were likewise affected by God's lessons in my journey.

Three days before the wedding, Lauren and I were discussing the meteorologist's warning of a cold front and thunderstorms for the weekend. My reputation as a shopper was not lost in this situation. This was something I could help with, right from my bed. I could contribute in this simple yet affirming way. I never imagined ordering fur wraps for the bridesmaids for an April wedding, but Texas weather is a guessing game at best. After confirming my order, accomplishment and joy rose higher than the circumstances surrounding me, having used my brain for something other than medical reports. The bottom line is that you can try to sideline a shopper, but she will rise to the occasion in a crunch.

PART EIGHT
Walking into the Beyond

"For we live by faith, not by sight."
2 Corinthians 5:7 (NIV)

18

Listen My Child

That night unfolded like all the others since being admitted to Butler Hospital. The nurses and technicians' routines remained the same. By now, Ralph and I had their schedules emblazoned in our brains. Sometimes I played a game with myself, trying to predict the exact time the next staffer would walk into my room. As days flowed into weeks, I got pretty good at it. I smiled as they entered the room at the time I predicted.

I must give credit where credit is due. My smile was also for the kindness the staff exhibited as they cared for me. Nurses and technicians work hard while receiving little appreciation or recognition. My mother's wise reminder never left me. "You can catch more flies with honey than you can with vinegar." No matter my mental state, I did my best to be kind, and they reciprocated.

Around nine o'clock, Ralph helped me get comfortable in bed. Pillow positioning after hours in bed was crucial to my comfort level. Hospital pillows scrunch differently. The struggle is real. Okay, maybe the pillow placement didn't guarantee sleep, but it allowed me reasonable comfort for staring at the ceiling or watching the clock advance.

Once I was settled, Ralph kissed me goodnight and retreated to his side of the room. It resembled what I imagine living in a tiny house to be like. The space included a couch-bed, desk, TV, and mini-kitchen. It provided space for him to rest and catch up on work when possible. With the room's lights lowered, I lay across the room watching Ralph, praying that God would sustain him. He had so much on his plate and was trying to carry the load alone. Tonight, weighed down by stress and exhaustion, his gentle snoring sounded better than it ever had to me.

Assuming this night would resemble the others, where sleep eluded me, I tuned into an episode of The Office. Nights were consumed by hours of staring at the ceiling and wrestling with my thoughts. Darkness draped the room as so many *would have* and *should have* thoughts flooded my mind.

"What should I have taught our children by this age?"

"How many times did I miss opportunities to tell them, Ralph, and other family members that I loved them?"

When we face even the possibility of death, reflective questions occupy more mental real estate than on normal days. Tonight, the unanswered questions in my mind stretched as wide as a football field. What did it mean that I was having these thoughts? Was God giving me a sign by speaking to me through my own words?

Like most Christians, I'm a work in progress—gripping God's hand tightly as I walk this journey. He has taught me much through study and trials, but undoubtedly, He wants to enhance my spiritual maturity through new experiences. Yes, I prayed for healing, but my prayers were varied. Sometimes, spoken boldly in peace. Other times, I whispered prayers while weeping into my pillow. In moments when I couldn't conjure up any words at all, I depended on God to read my heart.

In all honesty, when life pushes us to desperation, we can all admit to fear and questioning God. I certainly cried out in fear. We all also attest to easy faith in mountaintop seasons, but valley seasons are when the rubber meets the road. It's when what we say we believe is put to the test.

Our spiritual footprints become more defined with each trial. The same can be said for wrinkles and worry lines on our faces. They tell a story of what we've endured. God takes us through tough times to teach us dependence on Him. When we keep our focus on Him, He will strengthen our walk by deepening our faith.

As I look back on this entire experience, I am in awe of how God prepared me by strengthening my faith to new levels of spiritual maturity. If I had faced this situation ten years earlier, this baby Christian, who thought she had strong faith, would have folded under pressure with stronger cries of desperation.

God walked us through my father's two-year cancer journey and his subsequent death. He stood with us through other family deaths and crises as well. His presence was a constant pillar of faithfulness and strength that prepared me for my own date with destiny. Hindsight is described as twenty-twenty, but it's also a reminder and a gift of gratitude. Journaling allows me to reread entries of answered prayers and of God's steadfastness in my life. I am strengthened by the knowledge of things He's done for me, while also relying on Him to do them again, if it is His will.

God's lessons are revealed to us in various ways, sometimes determined by how mindful we are of Him. He is so many things to us, one of which is easily relatable to me. As a retired teacher, I can draw parallels between some of His teaching methods and those used in classrooms today.

When I wanted a student to do something, especially where their safety or that of others was in jeopardy, I had a progressive plan to achieve that goal.

First, I asked them nicely, "Would you please use your chair correctly, so you don't hurt yourself or anyone else?"

If that didn't work, I stated my expectation more directly, in a stronger tone and with direct eye contact. "Use your chair correctly."

If this didn't garner the correct response, I would position myself very close to the student and firmly insist on the correct behavior, along with an explanation of the consequences of non-compliance.

"If you don't use your chair correctly right now, you lose your chair for the next five minutes and your free time later today. Your parents will also receive a behavior notification."

Typically, by this point, the student had weighed his or her options against the consequences on which they knew I would not waiver. That usually resulted in compliance. But if not, as a last resort, I would write up a referral and escort the student to the principal's office for further discipline.

How must God feel when we do not comply with His

commands? As our Heavenly Father and teacher, surely, He is disappointed in many of our choices and behaviors. He loves us enough to want what is best for us and to teach us those things. If we choose alternate paths, He has ways to redirect us, ranging from a loving nudge to an extreme wake-up call. The more lenient the redirection, the more likely the preferred behavior will be postponed or ignored.

As God's guidance escalates into more direct lessons and directives, we often look for others to blame or an alternative to the situation. God doesn't enjoy disciplining His children any more than a loving parent does, but it is necessary at times.

As I lay wide-eyed, battling worrisome thoughts, God replaced my anxious breathing with familiar yoga breaths. Measured breaths released tension and grounded my body and my thoughts. Like a newborn whose days and nights are reversed, my occasional daytime naps of the last few weeks had sustained me but not revived me. In yet another attempt, I closed my eyes and prayed for the full night's sleep that had eluded me like a thief on the run.

Once again, the thief won, so there I lay, deep breathing and examining shadows cast by monitor lights and the slightly tilted blinds of the ICU nurse's window into my room. The familiar faint glow of my room at night, combined with the promise of hours of awake time, usually meant I had too much time to consider the seriousness of my condition. In those moments, the Holy Spirit's comfort came in the form of sweet visions of me with my family and friends. Nothing special. Just everyday moments that now held major significance. I thank

God for reminding me of my blessings and reasons to fight for my life.

Suddenly, a vacuum of darkness and silence overtook the room. Straining to detect any light source or the shadows I'd studied earlier, I was met with a veil of blackness and deafening silence. As my heart began pounding, sweat beads gathered on my forehead, and fear crept up my spine, exploding in my heart and spreading across my chest. Despite my legs being frozen in place, I slid my hand under the sheet and pinched myself—hard. The stinging pain was evidence enough for me to understand I was, in fact, awake.

Questions tangled in my mind like an unraveled skein of yarn at the mercy of a cat at play. Confusion overrode them all. Was I fainting? Was I dying? I had done a lot of talking about dying, but I honestly had no idea what the actual moment would feel like. Even the possibility that this might be God calling me home was more intense than anything I'd ever experienced. The moment was infused with holy gravity and trembling reverence.

My trembling hands gripped the cool bed rail, steadying me. I was still alive and not asleep. The comforting hug of my inflatable mattress was more assurance of that fact.

Wait! What's happening?

I can't feel my mattress anymore!

I opened my mouth to call Ralph, but was met with no voice, even though I was convinced that I had yelled. Ralph's steady breathing had faded into silence as time stood still. Slow, soft beats and calm breaths replaced the thunderous pounding of my heart like the peace of calm seas. The Holy Spirit's peace enveloped me like a welcome, overdue warm blanket. This peace was a gentle embrace, yet a more powerful peace than I had ever experienced in my life. No more questions. No more fear. Only His peace.

As I lay there enjoying my newfound peace, yet trying to make sense of my surroundings, which had disappeared, my trust in God was at a profoundly deeper and unexplainable level. Slowly, my body rose, weightless, above the bed. Instead of detachment, a deep spiritual awareness consumed me. I was suspended, perfectly horizontal, as if an unseen force had slid a board beneath me and lifted me skyward. The shaking hands and frozen legs no longer existed.

The inky blackness was no longer intimidating. Even though I was confused, God had kept His promise I'd read so many times in *John 14:27 (NIV):*

"Peace, I leave with you; my peace I give to you. I do not give to you as the world gives...Do not let your hearts be troubled, and do not be afraid."

Suddenly, all was revealed to me. Just as Saul saw a light from Heaven on his journey to Damascus and heard Jesus' command, the darkness of my room was pierced by a blinding light that beckoned me to stare into it, rather than avert my eyes.

As he neared Damascus on his journey, suddenly a light from Heaven flashed around him. He fell to the ground and heard a voice say to him, "Saul, Saul, why do you persecute me?" Acts 9:3-4 (NIV)

No description I'd ever read or heard compared to the brilliance and power of the light before me. Knowing that I was in the presence of my Heavenly Father, my focus was drawn directly toward it. Without any hesitation or thought about what to say or do, I spoke. "God, is that you?"

Silence echoed.

"Father in Heaven, please speak to me."

I heard nothing but my desperate cries to my Almighty Father. However, His peace welcomed me into His presence, offering precious love and mercy. The magnitude of being with the Lord engulfed me in visceral emotions. The flood of tears streaming down my face served as a reminder of the reality and the reverence of the moment.

I longed to see His face, but His light shining before me was awe-inspiring and beyond my imagination. The sacredness of this experience filled my soul and calmed all fear. Without concern for clarity or visible evidence, I basked in my Father's heavenly serenity, not knowing how long it would last or how it would end.

"I see you."

"I know your situation," the Lord reassured me.

The Lord saw into my very soul, whom He created. His clear, deep, and commanding voice pierced the silence. Listening intently in complete amazement, I hung on every word of our exchange.

"I love You, Lord! I trust You with my life." I cried out, "Will I be healed in Heaven with You? Are You taking me now?"

I was talking to my Lord, and even better, He was talking to me. Understanding that He was referring to my life-or-death situation was a blessing of comfort and peace. I waited breathlessly, uncertain of how much time I had in His presence and how He would reply.

"No, my child. You are going **back.** You will be healed **there."** His tone was commanding yet loving.

Before I go any further, let me emphasize two key words in God's answer. He referred to me going "back" and to me being healed "there." This confirmed any speculation of being transported to another realm but returning according to His Will. My soul was not in that hospital room, but rather in the presence of the Holiest of Holies.

19

Still in Business

Still in Business

I was going back! Back to my family and friends. Back to tell God's miracle story in my life. Hearing His life-changing words flooded me with emotion and the feeling of a caged bird being set free. I would live in freedom. I trusted in Him. In fact, I was excited to watch God work this liver thing out His way. He said it. I believed it. I was standing on His Word.

A flood of tears drenched my face, filtering the brilliant light as it began to fade. I could relax in the confidence of God's promise for my life. No fear. No more questioning. Our conversation in the Heavenlies was all the confirmation that I possibly needed.

I've had dreams and even hallucinations from anesthesia. This was no dream or hallucination. Nothing compared to knowing that my Lord met me in that hospital room. God had drawn me to Him, speaking clearly in His powerful, yet soothing voice.

My anointed experience with the Lord was transformative and nearly impossible to convey in human language. After such a profound encounter, transformative is the most powerful way I can describe it. When God met me in my valley and revealed glimpses of the mountaintop ahead of me, I was forever changed. I will sing His praises and tell His story until He brings me home. My prayers were for God to use me to glorify Him, so that others might see His love and power. I didn't know exactly how this would happen, but I held tightly to His Word that He had a plan for me.

Many books have been written about out-of-body experiences and encounters with God. Mine may differ greatly from the others, but I am compelled to share what I experienced and know to be true. The lyrics of John Reddick's song, "I Believe It," resonate in my soul because my story isn't simply a narrative. It's my testimony of God's miracle in my life. I am literally a walking testimony to His healing power revealed in my presence. Thank You, God, for loving each of us enough to meet us in our hour of need and for fulfilling Your Will in our lives.

Before I could comprehend what just happened, the firm pressure of my inflatable mattress against my back grounded me. The sheets and pillows' scent and texture were the same, but nothing would ever be the same for me. My Heavenly Father had called me into His presence and given me a glimpse behind the veil. He revealed His plan for me to be healed on earth. I didn't know how I would be healed, but I trusted Him completely. He said it. I believed it. How could I possibly be the same after the most powerful experience of my life?

Like a new day dawning, the room began to brighten to its

normal nighttime level. The monitors' glow and the lights from tall buildings outside peeked in, drawing me back to reality. My now loudly audible crying was enough to startle Ralph. This was further confirmation to me that when I thought I was calling to him or crying loudly, those sounds between God and me were sacred. Otherwise, Ralph would have woken up.

He was at my bedside in an instant. Finding me sitting up, sobbing uncontrollably, alarmed him and forced him out of his drowsy stupor. He pulled my trembling body to him. "What's wrong? Tell me what's wrong. Do we need to call the nurse?"

Initially, stunned and overwhelmed, shaking my head was my best attempt at signaling that we did not need to call for help. Between sobs, I managed to shove his hand away from the call button.

"I'm crying because I'm happy. I'm not in pain."

With confusion covering his face, Ralph asked, "What happened? What are you talking about? I still think we should have the nurse check you out."

"No! Please, just wait," I insisted. I struggled to calm myself enough to explain. Reluctantly, Ralph respected my plea and removed his hand from the call button.

"Just hold me, please."

After a few cleansing breaths and some water at Ralph's insistence, I did my best to tell him what I had just experienced. It was as difficult to put into words as it is now. He sat there holding me in awe and confusion as I carefully relived the details of my experience. Ralph supported me and allowed me to bask in the sacredness of my moment, rather than interrupt it with the questions that were, no doubt, overflowing in his mind.

Sitting in that dim, quiet ICU room, we prayed together, thanking God for His mercy and power. Tears of gratitude poured from our eyes as we held each other, neither wanting to disturb the peace blanketing the room. We appreciated the holiness of this moment.

I assured Ralph, yet again, that I was okay physically and didn't need a doctor or nurse. I feared that if I shared my experience with them, they would suspect that I wasn't lucid. I knew better. God knew better. Nothing had ever been clearer in my life than what I just experienced. We kept the experience to ourselves in the confidence that God would work it out for my good in His way and in His time. We would wait in joyful anticipation, claiming this promise from Romans:

"And we know that in all things God works for the good of those who love Him, who have been called according to His purpose." Romans 8:28 (NIV)

While waiting in anxious anticipation, Dr. Ash and his team entered my room for morning rounds. Ralph wasted no time positioning himself at my bedside so he could anchor me through and clasped hands. I silently prayed for good news.

Glancing at the wall clock, I noticed that Dr. Ash and his team were later than usual but thought little of it. The look on the usually stoic team members' faces told me they had some news. Deciding whether the news was negative or positive was the difficult part. We didn't have to wait long before Dr. Ash spoke.

"Mrs. Porter, I'm not quite certain what to make of your test results this morning or how to tell you this. After having your results reviewed by my colleagues for verification, we agree that your current liver numbers have reversed themselves and are now completely within the normal range."

Ralph and I glanced at each other and smiled as we squeezed each other's hands even tighter.

This was it! God was working it out for me!

A scripture from one of Grandmother Sadie's walks with me rose up I my soul. We'd talked about getting old and sick when Grandmother shared this verse:

"Nevertheless, I will bring health and healing to it; I will heal my people and will let them enjoy abundant peace and security." Jeremiah 33:6 (NIV)

As God promised the people of Judah healing and restoration in Jerusalem's devastation, God had performed a physical healing for my devastated body. Hallelujah!

"We cannot explain to you how this happened, but the numbers do not lie. I want to continue running your labs throughout the day to confirm our findings. If the results remain consistent, you may be going home soon. In the meantime, you will remain in this room, but I will downgrade you to regular status, as opposed to ICU level. I appreciate that this all probably seems unbelievable. Trust me, Mrs. Porter. We are just as amazed as you are right now. Do you have any questions for me?"

Through teary eyes, I stared at Dr. Ash, but my thoughts were of earlier that morning when I stared into the light and heard my Heavenly Father's voice. God is still in the miracle business. He kept His promise. Tears found their path down my cheeks as I shook my head. I had no questions. God had answered them all.

"In that case, we'll go over today's lab results and make decisions in the morning based on them. You take care and have a wonderful day, Mrs. Porter."

Part of me begged to shout to the Heavens and tell everyone, but another part was more comfortable holding my encounter with the Father close to my heart. My experience was a physically life-changing experience, combined with a spiritual one as well. God had given me a second chance at life. I was a new person, and that was worth cherishing.

God deserved all the glory and honor that I could possibly give Him now and forever. I gave it to Him privately, uncertain as to how to glorify Him publicly. One thing I did know was that sooner or later, people would need to hear or read my testimony. It is a message of hope and confirmation of God's healing power. He did miracles during biblical times, and He still does them today. He is loving and faithful. Nothing on this earth can deter His plans for each of us.

The message in my miracle is for others battling life-threatening diagnoses or other dire circumstances. Our job is to remain in a deep relationship with God and always aspire to live in His Will.

The power of our own prayers and that of intercessors could not be denied. I was blessed by so many family members, friends, and even friends of friends, praying for me and standing in solidarity with me, trusting God's mercy. I will forever be indebted to every one of them for their faithfulness. He hears the prayers of the faithful.

"Therefore, confess your sins to each other and pray for each other so that you may be healed. The prayer of a righteous person is powerful and effective." James 5:1(NIV)

I don't know whether it was the impact of my experience meeting God or the relief of His promise fulfilled, but exhaustion hit me hard. After battling sleep every night since admission, I slept between every blood draw all day. Not just trusting but knowing that my God had worked a miracle in my body. He blessed me with a deeper appreciation for that peace beyond understanding that I'd read in scripture and heard my elders speak about.

Ralph and I settled in for the night, hopeful that the morning would bring more good news. God gave us both a peaceful night's rest, which we thanked Him for during our morning prayer. We were freshened up and waiting when Dr. Ash walked in. As usual, he wasted no time.

With a smile, he asked me, "Would you like to go to your daughter's wedding? I can confidently ask you that question now.

These were words from Heaven straight to my ears. If I had the strength, I would have jumped out of bed and hugged that man.

"We feel confident in discharging you, but you will need to be monitored weekly, then monthly, to be certain your liver is functioning properly. This can be done from a lab in your hometown. You will need to take it easy for quite some time. Today, though, you are cleared to attend your daughter's wedding. How does that sound to you?"

My reply came easily this time. "It sounds like a miracle to me, Dr. Ash."

PART NINE

Walking in His Purpose

"For I know the plans I have for you,' declares the Lord,
'plans to prosper you and not to harm you,
plans to give you hope and a future."
Jeremiah 29:11 (NIV)

20

New Day Dawning

I was downright giddy and could not wait another minute to let my family know that I was being discharged. Shocked doesn't begin to describe their reactions to the surprising news. Understandably, each one pressed me with questions, trying to make it make sense. Promising to answer them all later, I hopped off the phone so Ralph could help me get dressed and packed.

Tameko arrived just in time, wearing a huge smile and smothering me in an even bigger hug. She and Ralph worked out a plan to get me out of there and to free Ralph up to do one more road trip back home for last-minute wedding items.

After waiting almost two hours for discharge orders to clear, Tameko drove me to Mom's house in Dallas. I love and appreciate how perceptive she is. Even though I'm sure she had as many questions as our children, she remained quiet during the ride, allowing me some to take in the feeling of sunshine on my face and the joy in my heart.

Mom met me on her doorstep, embracing me in the kind of warm, sweet hug I'd cherished since infancy. Then, she insisted that I get into my pajamas and relax in bed. I was more than happy to oblige her. The bigger bed and soft sheets engulfed me like a cloud. It wasn't long before I drifted off to sleep.

As I opened my eyes, it took a minute to realize that I wasn't in the hospital anymore. That prompted a little happy dance in bed. Next came the aroma of something delicious wafting into the guest room. Mom's chicken and dumplings, one of my favorites, made my heart smile. I wanted to slip out of bed and go to the kitchen.

I could hear Tameko and Mom talking as I pulled on my robe and made my way as far as the living room . Met with shocked expressions, Tameko hurried to help me settle into a chair.

"I feel okay except for being a little weak. I promise."

"If you feel okay, do you want to try to eat something?" Mom offered.

"What do you think got me out of that comfy bed? I would recognize the scent of your chicken and dumplings anywhere."

Encouraged by the lack of immediate queasiness, I didn't want to overdo it and get sick. After a few tentative sips of the broth, I forged ahead and enjoyed half a bowl before stopping. I wanted more but didn't dare refill my bowl. Just a few hours ago, I was in a hospital bed. Now Tameko, Mom, and I sat at her table. The food, laughter, and love were reminiscent of old times. All I could think was, "God is so good."

Meanwhile, Ralph was on his way back from Abilene for the last time before the big day. At this point, we were two days out from the wedding. Plans were coming together, according to Lauren and Ralph. Unfortunately, even though I wanted to feel connected to it all, my body was in control, and it needed rest. I slept most of the day and the next.

Before I knew it, my cousin Sherry was at Mom's door to drive me to the wedding host hotel. Unbeknownst to me, Raph arranged for Sherry to get me to the hotel while he helped Rae unload and inventory wedding décor. Sherry had her own questions about how I managed to get discharged after being at the brink of a transplant or worse.

"It was a miracle from God."

As a believer, she was readily accepting of the idea that God works in His own time.

Arriving at the hotel symbolized things coming to fruition. As adults, we sometimes miss moments because we don't focus on the present. Instead, we're usually thinking ahead to the next thing. I did my best to soak in every tiny moment as the beautiful gifts they were to me. Just pulling into the hotel parking lot brought chill bumps to my arms and legs, but God had made it so. I knew our family and friends would be inside or arriving soon. This was exciting, but this little road trip across the metroplex had exhausted me.

Sherry and I bypassed the incoming guests at the front desk and headed straight to the elevator up to the suite. Ralph had checked in, so Sherry got me settled in the room easily. After I politely refused her offer to get me food, I slid into the second non-hospital bed in two days.

Restlessly stirring in the bed, my mind automatically defaulted to my time surrounded by beeping monitors and the pungent scent of commercial cleansers. Even through my eyelids, the harshness of fluorescent lighting was no longer battling for my consciousness.

Thank God Almighty!

I was surrounded by the beautiful décor of a hotel suite, the very one that Lauren, Rae, and I had toured and booked months earlier for this occasion. The rehearsal dinner day had arrived, and so did I. Reverently, I thanked God for His miracle work in my life.

Quentin's parents had planned the rehearsal dinner in one of the hotel's banquet rooms. I was grateful it was just downstairs. The theme was western, so when Ralph returned to the hotel, he and I did our best to transform my now frail body into a cowgirl for the evening. My makeup hid a multitude of flaws. My highlighted, contoured face declared *party*, while my body begged for rest. The added weight loss during hospitalization was seriously obvious once I got into my clothes. They swallowed me like an adult outfit on a baby hanger. None of that mattered, though. It was time to celebrate.

Once inside the banquet room, family and friends surrounded me with hugs and well-wishes. Understanding that I was still weak and lightheaded, Ralph's first priority was to get me seated at our table.

As proud parents, we watched with immense joy as Quentin and Lauren were honored as the bride and groom-to-be. I could feel God in the blessing of their union. In those moments, reflection and gratitude took precedence over celebration. Silent prayers were offered before I turned my heart and mind back to the occasion at hand.

By the time the program ended and the music was cranked up, guests began mingling. I smiled through the familiar nausea that the food reprised. Hugging guests and retelling my hospital experience repeatedly exhausted me more than I expected. Recognizing my limitations, I asked Ralph to help me back upstairs to rest. With the attentiveness of a private nurse, he had me settled for the night in minutes. I couldn't wait to dream about the wedding day.

21

The Big Day

The bridal party was tasked to be at the wedding venue early Saturday morning to rehearse. Ralph headed downstairs to grab some breakfast before meeting them there. He found family and friends already eating while searching online for the closest stores. Everyone was scurrying to buy coats, scarves, and umbrellas to prepare for the cold front that arrived overnight. Some shopped online while others sent money and requests, along with shoppers hitting the stores. No one was ignoring the fact that by early evening, the temperature would be even colder and possibly wet.

After an entire morning of resting and reading, a knock at the door delivered Rae's surprise: soup and bread. Rae thought of everything—even caring for me while running a rehearsal. I was strong enough to sit at the table and enjoy my lunch. Ralph texted updates, checking on me and asking where certain décor items were. According to his updates, the venue was buzzing with activity.

As if there hadn't been at least fifty wedding decisions made, Quentin and Lauren had a huge one to make today. When I toured venues with them months ago, this one matched their vision. The hilltop villa, with its outdoor gazebo and cross, was the perfect backdrop for their wedding. The villa itself was taken from the pages of a romance novel. The keyword here is "outdoor" in the cold, rainy weather.

Rae rehearsed both the indoor and outdoor setups. No one knew what the next hours would bring but God. In the end, Quentin and Lauren chose to stick with their original outdoor vision.

With that decision made, it was time for hair and makeup. Hair stylists and makeup artists arrived on-site to work their magic while the groomsmen, ushers, and dads enjoyed the rest of the day relaxing. These were moments they would treasure forever, rooted in this verse:

Therefore, shall a man leave his father and his mother and cleave unto his wife, and they shall become one flesh. Genesis 2:24 (KJV)

The makeup artist had her work cut out for me. My ski was still a bit jaundiced, and the dark circles under my eyes were like dark craters sunken in my gaunt face. For this reason, Lauren explained my situation to the makeup artist and allowed more time for her to work her magic on me. She managed to transform me into a refreshed, put-together mother of the bride rather than one who had been released from the hospital two days prior. When she spun me around to face her big mirror, my spirits lifted.

"Thank you. Thank you." I kept repeating as I took in my reflection. The last thing I wanted was to look sick and become the center of attention due to concern for my health. This was Quentin and Lauren's big day, not mine.

My dress, once a perfect fit, now allowed room for thermals against the cold. Despite my condition, I thanked God for bringing me through to witness our daughter marry the love of her life. Today was an anticipated celebration coming to fruition because of His mercy and power. No matter how threatening life's trials may feel, trust our Savior who holds all the power and loves us beyond our imagination.

As directed by Ralph and Rae, I rested in a quiet room upstairs until my cue to come down. No matter how hard I fought it, anticipation got the best of me. There was no way I could turn off my thoughts to relax. It was time to stand up for Quentin and Lauren and to let everyone know God is good and on His throne.

As soon as I appeared at the top of the same staircase, Ralph and Ryan noticed me. To this day, I find myself returning to the picture the photographer captured of Ralph looking up at me lovingly before he rushed up to assist me down. It was a beautiful moment between the two of us, but also a reminder of how our God waits for us to reach out to Him. He wants to take our hand and help us. He is patiently waiting on us to make a move toward Him. Often, we hesitate in reaching out to God because we believe He wants grand gestures from us. Don't hesitate. Just call His name. Take a tiny step. He will meet you where you are.

Downstairs, friends hugged me with whispered encouragement as they huddled near the massive fireplace. I was overwhelmed with well-wishes.

"We prayed for you."

"I'm so thankful you were able to be here today."

Each comment was heartfelt, and I received them with much gratitude. When others commented on how lucky I was to be there, without hesitation, I corrected them, explaining this was not luck, but God's mercy, grace, and miracle-working power. Some gave confused looks and just nodded, while others were brought back to their own faith and realization of what God had done in their lives.

Soon, Rae invited guests to take their seats, and bundled in coats, they moved outside. Taking a last look around the venue at the assembled wedding party, my heart overflowed. Rae had them lined up and waiting for their cues to proceed down the aisle. It was time.

Quentin and Lauren were waiting to step into their new life together. This was their big day, and I was blessed to be healthy enough to witness it. I was reminded of God's arms that wrapped me in love and grace every day on this journey. This weather had nothing on my God. He had brought me through so many storms in life to the point of healing my body. This was a time to rejoice, even if it was through chattering teeth.

Ryan looked as handsome in his tuxedo as his wife, Caitlin, looked beautiful in her bridesmaid's dress. This was one of so many proud moments of the wedding experience. My family knows that making memories is extremely important to me. I always pray to be present in them, rather than distracted. Taking a deep breath, I took in the moment.

Insisting that I wear my coat down the aisle, Ryan felt better once I assured him I would put it on after I got to my seat. "Plus, I'm wearing thermals," I whispered.

So many thoughts flooded my mind in those last few seconds before I was drawn back to reality with a nudge from Ryan.

"Ready, Mom?"

He offered his arm. I whispered one last prayer of thanks. God had healed me, and now I was in the moment that I thought was lost to me. Ryan and I walked into the brisk spring air and into my future as a forever grateful, healed daughter of the King.

Epilogue

The soothing aroma of coffee and the soft background soundtrack in my favorite coffee shop are interrupted by the clicking of laptop keys. With a never-ending smile, I excitedly pour my thoughts and experiences onto the backlit page. I am writing my healing testimony story. It runs parallel to Quentin and Lauren's wedding story. Amid such joy, none of us could have predicted my harrowing, then divine health journey.

I returned home after the wedding weekend and set up my liver monitoring through a local lab. After seven years of monitoring my liver function and consistently getting normal results, I am reminded every day when I wake up on this side of Heaven, just how blessed I am and how much hope God can give others through my story. Those who see me but don't know my story would have no idea that I faced death, BUT I also faced God and heard His miraculous words of hope for my life.

Mom died of complications from dementia two years after my healing. Lauren and I got matching tattoos of hers and our favorite hymn: "It Is Well." Every time the tattoo catches my eye, God's peace washes over me. Her immeasurable faith, passed down from Grandmother Sadie, motivates me daily to emulate her level of obedience to God.

As a writer, my list of potential book ideas has grown over the years. Some of them have instead found their way into individual pieces of poetry, and others into talks I've shared with small Christian groups. Other ideas wait to be cued up and transformed into whatever God leads me toward. This story, though, was particularly blessed and anointed by the Holy Spirit.

God is many things, and one of those is persistent. If you have a relationship with Him, you already know this. We can turn away from His urging, but at some point, our plans will falter, and His will prevail if we are faithful and obedient to Him. He will use whatever measures are necessary to direct our attention toward His plan. In my case, He used scriptures and sermons that pierced my heart, as if they were explicitly for me. You may have experienced similar moments when God's Words seem laser-focused on your problems, and the world around you falls. This is when that same scripture or sermon others are simultaneously hearing becomes a message delivered directly to your soul.

Testing the waters to get a feel for how my testimony would be received was important to me. I began sharing an abbreviated version of it every opportunity I had, and it was met with positive responses. In fact, many suggested that I write this book.

After a while, though, others' opinions didn't matter

anymore. God showed me that writing my testimony would be an act of obedience by leading me to the following scripture.

And God is able to bless you abundantly, so that in all things at all times, having all that you need, you will abound in every good work. 2 Corinthians 9:8 (NIV)

God doesn't call us to something to leave us to fend for ourselves. He asks that we are willing. He is with us, and He enables us to finish the assignment. Each time I prayerfully approach my keyboard, battling the fear and inadequacy lies of imposter syndrome, He calls me to embrace His promise to see the project through to completion for His kingdom purpose. I am unable to ignore His voice saying these simple words.

"Tell it! Write it!" So here I sit trusting God word by word.

Throughout this process, God has shown me just how faithful He is as my anchor. My biggest takeaways from my miracle healing and this writing project are:

- When the world says you can't do it, GOD CAN. Believe it.

Those seven little words "...nothing we can do for you here," weren't a death sentence, but instead an opportunity for God to display His power in my life.

- Acknowledge and obey God's urgings. He will equip you for His purpose. Look at me. I know my

> testimony better than anyone else. He replaced my fear with stronger faith. He showed me that I can do hard things when I stay in a close relationship with Him, and SO CAN YOU.

I understand that you may be reading this book from a place that doesn't include a relationship with Christ. In that case, I applaud you for making it this far. I also encourage you not to be dismissive. Your natural mind may not completely understand and appreciate spiritual concepts until you establish a deep relationship with the Lord. I can't in good conscience continue without inviting you to get to know Him for yourself. If you ask the Lord into your heart, He will come in, and the door to a deeper relationship will swing wide open. Step in, dear one. Reach for His hand. He will take yours and walk with you through whatever life brings. Your future may hold sickness or other forms of stress. In fact, God tells us that we will experience trouble in our lives. The good news is that He will never leave you. If you trust Him, He will walk you through whatever you trials you face. With the Lord, you can experience His love and mercy, which is truly beyond all understanding.

This book was written to edify and praise God. I will forever share my miracle healing experience. Everyone needs to know that people like me exist in this world, going about our daily lives. The Lord still heals bodies, hearts, and situations. I pray that my book lands in the hands of those who need this promise of hope from God. He has been and will always be my anchor and my firm foundation. He waits patiently to walk with you and be yours, as well.

Amen

Scripture List

Exodus 4:10-12 (NIV)

1 Corinthians 6:19 (NIV)

1 Corinthians 10:31 (NIV)

Galatians 6:2 (NIV)

John 15:5 (NIV)

Matthew 25:40 (NIV)

Proverbs 17:17 (NIV)

Acts 13:2-3 (NIV)

Philippians 4:6-7 (NIV)

Deuteronomy 31:6 (NIV)

1 Corinthians 12:25 (NIV)

Psalm 39:4 (NIV)

2 Thessalonians 3:16 (NIV)

Psalm 139:4 (NIV)

Psalm 16:8 (KJV)

Acts 13:2-3 (NIV)

Isaiah 53:1 (NIV)

Psalm 39:7 (NIV)

Isaiah 40:31 (NIV)

Romans 8:28 (NIV)

Jeremiah 33:6 (NIV)

James 5:1(NIV)

Genesis 2:24 (KJV)

2 Corinthians 9:8 (NIV)

Exodus 20:12 (NIV)

1 Peter 4:8 (NIV)

James 5:16 (KJV)

Luke 6:31(NIV)

Philippians 4:13 (NIV)

Colossians 3:14 (NIV)

Psalm 23:4 (NIV)

Hebrews 13:16 (NIV)

Jeremiah 29:11 (NIV)

Hebrews 10:36 (NIV)

Colossians 3:13 (NIV)

Hebrews 6:19-20 (NIV)

Psalm 39:7 (NIV)

Ecclesiastes 3:1 (KJV)

Psalm 37:23 (NIV)

Jeremiah 6:16 (NIV)

2 Corinthians 5:7 (NIV)

A Closing Prayer for You

Heavenly Father,

Thank You for giving me this testimony to share. You knew my purpose before You created me. I've watched You line up events and decisions that have led to me sharing Your powerful miracle in my life with readers.

Thank You for walking with the reader through every page of my testimony. I pray that You met them on these pages and spoke truth and hope to them. You are a sovereign God who sees, knows, and guides all of us if we'll only listen and obey. I believe that You brought the reader to Walking in Grace. It was no accident that they chose my book, whether they realized it or not. Father, may my testimony of Your goodness reveal You, Your love, and Your power.

If they finished my book with unanswered questions and prayers, I ask You to meet them right where they are. Fill them with hope for the hopeless times; light when the road ahead seems long and uncertain; and strength where exhaustion has resided for so long.

Father, remind them that their struggle is not in vain and that You are with them always. Give them the faith to trust that

Your work beyond the veil will be revealed in Your time, and that the waiting is worth it

Teach the reader to walk in grace, especially when answers seem hidden or delayed. May they take refuge in You, Father. May they know You as their Savior, but also as their Healer, and their Restorer.

I pray that the reader will release whatever they're holding onto and place it into Your capable hands. You've promised that You will be faithful to complete the works You've begun in each of us. I stand on that promise for all of us.

May we all walk forward in grace, trusting You with every step.

In Your precious Son, Jesus' name,

Amen

Family Pictures

Robert and Sadie Barton, circa 1918

Pamela and Ralph at Ryan and Caitlin's wedding

Fit Camp workout

Lauren and Pamela at the Susan G. Komen 3-Day Walk

Puzzle time with Caitlin, Ryan, and Mom

My sister, Tameko

Quentin and Lauren attending a wedding

Pamela and Ryan at Quentin and Lauren's wedding

Lauren and Quentin after their wedding vows

My beloved family: Ryan, Caitlin, Cameron, Landon, Lauren, Noa, Quentin, Pamela, Ralph

Thank You!

Thanks for reading Walking in Grace. If you found my book helpful, your review will help others find my book easier. Please go to Amazon or wherever you bought the book and leave me a review today. Your feedback!

Thank you!!!

Let's Connect!

Instagram: @messybiblefullheart

Facebook: Pam Sneed Porter

About the Author

Pamela Porter has been passionate about reading and writing since she filled the pages of her first poetry notebook as a fourth-grade assignment. That early spark ignited a lifelong love of words and stories.

She spent 35 years as a devoted elementary school teacher, where she chose to invest her heart and energy into inspiring young children to discover the joy of reading and the power of writing.

Outside the classroom, Pamela has lived a rich and fulfilling life with her husband and their two children. She has been active supporting her church youth group and now enjoys the fellowship of her church friends and her marriage ministry group. In retirement, she embraced her most cherished role yet —GiGi. Now she enjoys traveling with her husband, showering love on her three grandchildren, and finding quiet moments to sip tea, read good books, and write from the heart.

WALKING IN GRACE is a story that God spoke into existence. It is a deeply personal testimony of faith, healing, and the power of God's promises in the most uncertain of times.

Made in the USA
Coppell, TX
19 February 2026

72353297R00106

For Keith.
Your wild joy and raucous happiness,
your faith and courageous heart
during brushes with life's darkest colors,
and your selfless dedication and compassionate
caring for so many people over the years
beautifully portray the landscape of living.

You are my favorite work of art—
the quintessence of a masterpiece.

Also for my grand-treasures.
Oh, always remember the joy and deep love
I have for you!

A heartfelt thank you to . . .

Keith, Barbara & James, John, Nilmini & Taylor,
Laura & Fletcher, Emily & Tommy, Natalie, Susan
& Verne, Becky, Cherie, Jane, Tod,
Stan, Terry, Mark, Stephen, Dean, Chris,
Spokane Poetry Scribes,
River Ridge Association of Fine Arts,
Spokane Watercolor Society,
South Hill Writers Group,
Spokane Authors and Self-publishers,
Lorna Johnson Print,
and all the rest who thoughtfully gave
contributions, critiques, and encouragement,
and who graciously provide opportunities
to share/learn/perform poetry and art.

And thank you God . . . always for You.

LILACS

Oil

The Lilac Painter

The painter of the Lilac bloom
Will fill an artist's palette soon
With luscious colors she believes
Can best create its flowers and leaves.

The Lilac City's heritage,
So gracing hills and under bridge.
It thrives in gardens, grand and small,
And sways beside the waterfall.

Remembering the festive times
Of Lilac queens and poets' rhymes,
The artist starts with brush in hand
To paint the flowers which dot our land.

Now captured in the vibrant bloom
Are hues of Ivory and Maroon.
And other colors, name by name,
Will celebrate its local fame.

The painter adds Deep Hookers Green,
And Terre Verte, Serpentine.
Some Sap and Olive blended in
With Yellow and Viridian.

Rose Madder, Pink, Vermillion Hue,
Magenta and Dark Purple, too,
And Violet, Fuchsia, Lavender.
A palette most spectacular!

The brush continues at its play
Upon the canvas for display.
A love for Lilacs, from the heart,
Reveals itself within the art.

A touch of hospitality—
The artist paints a cup for tea.
Immersed in scent, sweet Lilac cup.
Rich, perfumed blossoms fill you up.

Cascading 'round the saucer, too.
Imagine just a Lilac brew.
Then highlights left in sparingly
Will hold the light for you to see.

Some whisper strokes of Creamy Buff,
And blackened accents, just enough,
Can make the flowers pop and shine,
Reflecting petals in their prime.

Then Lilac painter steps away
To view the artful, sweet bouquet.
So grateful for the Master's touch,
And for the bloom she loves so much.

Oil

Empress Lilac Spring Debut

Lilac Double Blossom

Oil

Oil

Lilac Love Letter

Love that swirls in scented space.
Luscious Lilacs. Latticed vase
Circled by a golden base.
Painting tenderness and grace.

Intertwined with years of growth.
Sealed by our promised oath.
Memories when to you betroth.
Lilac letter to us both.

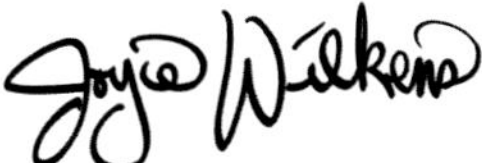

Lilac Swing

His drape is quite an orchestration.
"Off the cob," he says.
And he can jam and jive-a-plenty.
Swinging's just the mezz!

He spins the fragrant Lilac. See her
Swirling, whirling hem,
For she's the lovely dancing flower.
He—supportive stem.

They swing into a celebration.
Showcasing the town,
The youth and honored military.
Lilac blooms abound.

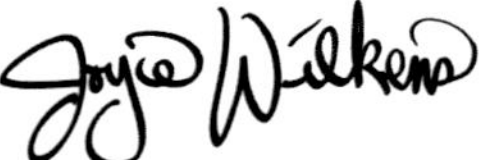

Oil

Old Bottles

Bottles from the distant past.
Green and white and orange glass.
For their beauty, light and shape,
Sometimes for the tones they make,
Or to challenge painters' eyes,
Folks collect them, every size.

Watercolor

A Painting's Story

Inside every painting waits a story to be told.
So as you gaze upon this piece, what story will unfold?

Take some quiet minutes viewing large and small details,
And think about what's happening here. A story then unveils.

Do her eyes betray her thoughts of circumstances grim?
Of growing disappointment as she calmly waits for him?

Did her one true love become a casualty of war
Or chancing this first meeting after letters shore to shore?

Are the flowers there to signal that she'd like to be
The wife of whom she's written to for months across the sea?

Where might she be waiting in a dress and faded hat?
She holds some lacy flowers as she waits to have a chat.

What could she be looking at? A clerk, a couple, child?
A fancy dress that's in the window of the mercantile?

Is some sickness plaguing her? She'll share the news with tears.
Or maybe some uncertainty about the one who hears?

Maybe calming thoughts about her future in the palm
Of one she calls her Father, now her soul's most soothing balm.

So as you've viewed and thought about what story just might be,
You've done what some may know as Visual Thinking Strategy.

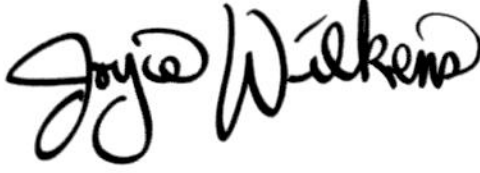

Artists: Becky Gromlich, Joy Gruenewald, Jane Wilson, Timothy Ely, Timothy Ely, Mari Anne Figgins, Michele Davis, Patty Jorgenson.

Artists: Sue Rohrback, Nilmini Wilkens, Matthew Pierce, Linda Smith, Diana Postlewait, Joyce Wilkens, Cherie Galusha, Anita Herdner, Dian Zahner, Joyce Wilkens.

Artists: Megan Perkins, Laura Wilkens, Caryn Adaryn, Bari Federspiel, Linda Smith, Abdul Al-Rais, Kay West, Lian Zhen, Vicki A. West.

Artists: Kim Merritt, Cynthia Stephan, Kim Merritt, Connie Janney, Tom Quinn, Martha Mason, Thomas Morphis.

Artists: Kurt Schmierer, Daniel Lopez, Sister Paula Turnbull (83 years old), Emily Poole, Stan Miller, Ken Spiering.

Art Abandoned

Places random, art abandoned.
Some astonished eyes.
It's not so rare to find somewhere
A hidden art surprise.

In grocery cart there may be art.
Behind a rock or tree.
Among the stacks or magazine racks
At the college library.

Why such pleasure, leaving treasure?
Artist's giving spree.
The joy and smiles across the miles
When finding art for free!

And there she rests. Our lives were blessed.
These flowers under glass,
Frame memories of my granny sweet
And linger in the grass.

Hope is spoken at a time
When loved ones then are gone.
For in this place we ponder them.
Eternity beyond.

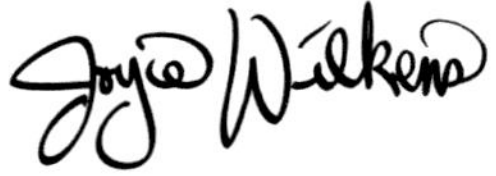

Framed watercolor collage abandoned at the Mt. Hope Cemetery, College Place, WA. This poem, posted on social media, gave clues to the whereabouts of this art piece. Collage pieces painted by 8th graders and artist. Assembled and watercolor/ ink pen enhanced by artist.

A Still Life?

Oil

If you were to ask me
"What is happening here?"
I'd take the time to contemplate
And see what becomes clear.

This is not a still life.
I see movement there.
A pesky fly is walking on
The second yellow pear.

Softly wind is blowing.
This is how I know.
The folds along the tablecloth
Are angled back just so.

Flowers nod in rhythm.
Glassy water bends
Their twisted, woody tendrils and
Impressionistic stems.

On a fragrant flower,
Inchworm might not think
He's flirting with disaster as
He hangs above the drink.

Watermelon slices
Lure a honey bee.
So are there any other signs
Of movement that you see? Yes!

WILDFLOWERS

Watercolor

Watercolor

Lily, Poppy, Pansy, too,
Begin this wild creation.
Daisy, Orchid, Mallow, Pink,
Complete this flower sensation,
Growing only in the soil
Of your imagination.

Watercolor

The delicate dance of bee and bloom.
A symbiotic song in tune.
Sweet buzzle, nuzzle love affair,
Until the gardener comes to prune.

Oil

TEA

Afternoon Tea Across America

There is a group of connoisseurs
Across America
Who savor teas from England and
The wilds of Africa.

From Europe, China and Japan,
Sri Lanka, Asia, too,
These teas that grow in distant lands,
The connoisseurs will brew.

And on the web you'll find these folks
Form great camaraderie.
They share exquisite teacups or
A tea time recipe.

Oil

A table set with fancy flair.
There's friendship from the heart.
They recommend some lovely books
Like one called *Teacup Art!*

And with a "welcome!" from this group
You might just like to see
Agendas for your afternoons
Include a cup of tea.

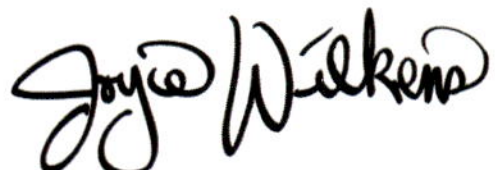

Oil

Fuchsia Dance

Oh, Fuchsia, come and dance with me.
The stage is set for morning tea.
Let's pirouette until we hear
The whistling teapot coming near.

Watercolor

Oil

The Days of Tea and Roses

A lazy breeze now ambles down
The path we used to walk.
It whispers cherished memories
Of love and garden talk.

You'd renamed all the roses, ha,
Like Bling or Humpty Dee!
So lightened by your laughter as
We sipped our morning tea.

Oil

My love for you shall long prevail
And time will not undo
The days of tea and roses . . .
And you.

Joyce Wilkens

Watercolor

Rescue

Teatime gives me ponder.
How can the earth survive?
It needs a crucial rescue soon
To save this fragile life.

What could tip the balance,
Or what could sink the scale
For want of human kindness and
Compassion not prevail?

Money—muddled market.
Lost freedom then to heed
One's mind and heart convictions—
Shouting universal creed?

Starving, crying hunger.
The power struck from grid.
Computers crashing. Unleashed anger.
Prejudice once hid.

Casually we "hate" things.
A common, spoken word.
But are we losing focus now?
Compassion's picture blurred.

Controversy building.
The routes that some travail.
Exhausted, tear-stained, anxious steps.
A slashed and ripped-up sail.

Terror-shaken cities.
The weather-torn-up lands.
Predictions for some seismic quakes.
Arthritic, begging hands.

What could tip the balance,
Or what could break the scale
For want of human kindness and
Compassion not prevail?

Yes, I savor beauty,
Which surely can be found
In sunsets or creative works—
A baby's babble sound.

Tainted, though, love's painted.
The mixed-up gallery.
The soul needs much enhancing by
An artist's mastery.

Did our earthly darkness
Originate beyond
The stunning, star-clad universe—
Sometime before the dawn?

Books and movies show it—
A conflict out in space,
When love so pleaded harmony,
But jealousy displaced.

History of a war then.
Earth's time had not begun.
Great controversy, cosmos wide,
But says a victor's won!

Shall I join a chorus,
When earth makes finished run?
Will churning clouds just split the sky
To welcome in a Son?

Watercolor

What could tip the balance?
Our gnarled, suffering strife.
I wait a gracious rescue soon
And gift of brand new life.

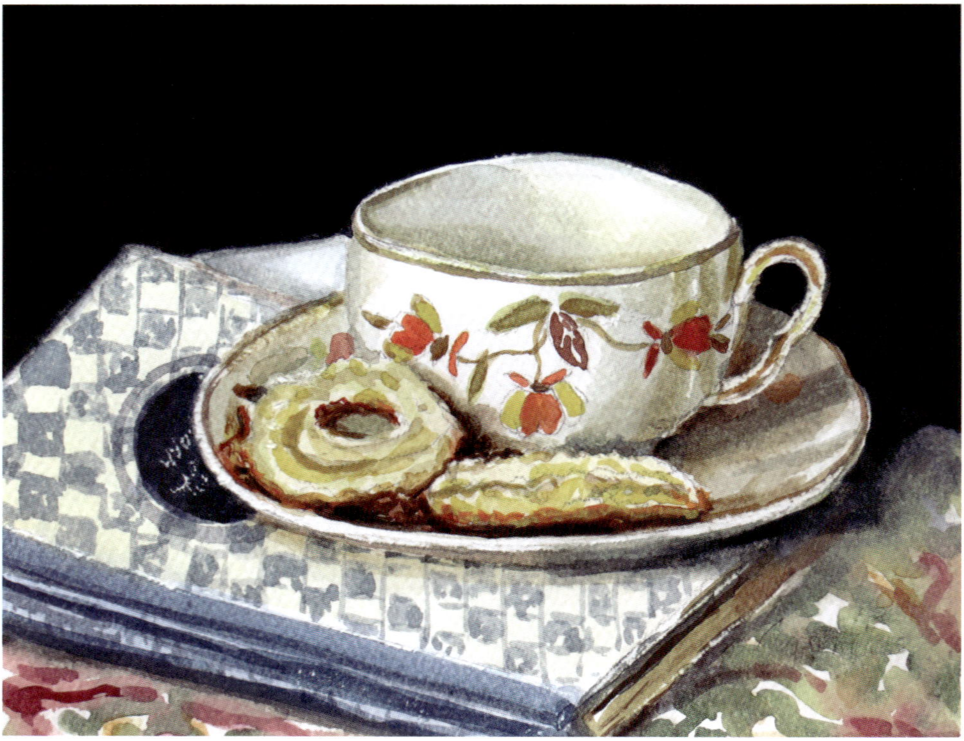

Watercolor

Winter's Tea

Golden, buttery **Swedish** Spritz,
Swedish recipe.
Scent of almond extract swirls.
Grandma's Jewel Tea.
Forest Spruce are **dusted** now,
Dusted white with snow.
Fire beckons at the hearth.
That's where I will go.
Grab a book . . . tranquility.
Perfect time for winter's tea.

Joyce Wilkens

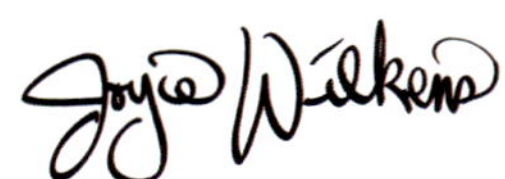

Watercolor

Two mothers laid their Springtime gifts
Each in their own fine nest.
Respecting their diversity,
They both were greatly blessed.

But then one saw a tragedy.
She with misfortune met.
And this I am quite certain of—
The cat had no regret.

(cont.)

To save the orphaned treasures now,
Cupped in my careful hands,
I place them in the foster home.
The sight is truly grand.

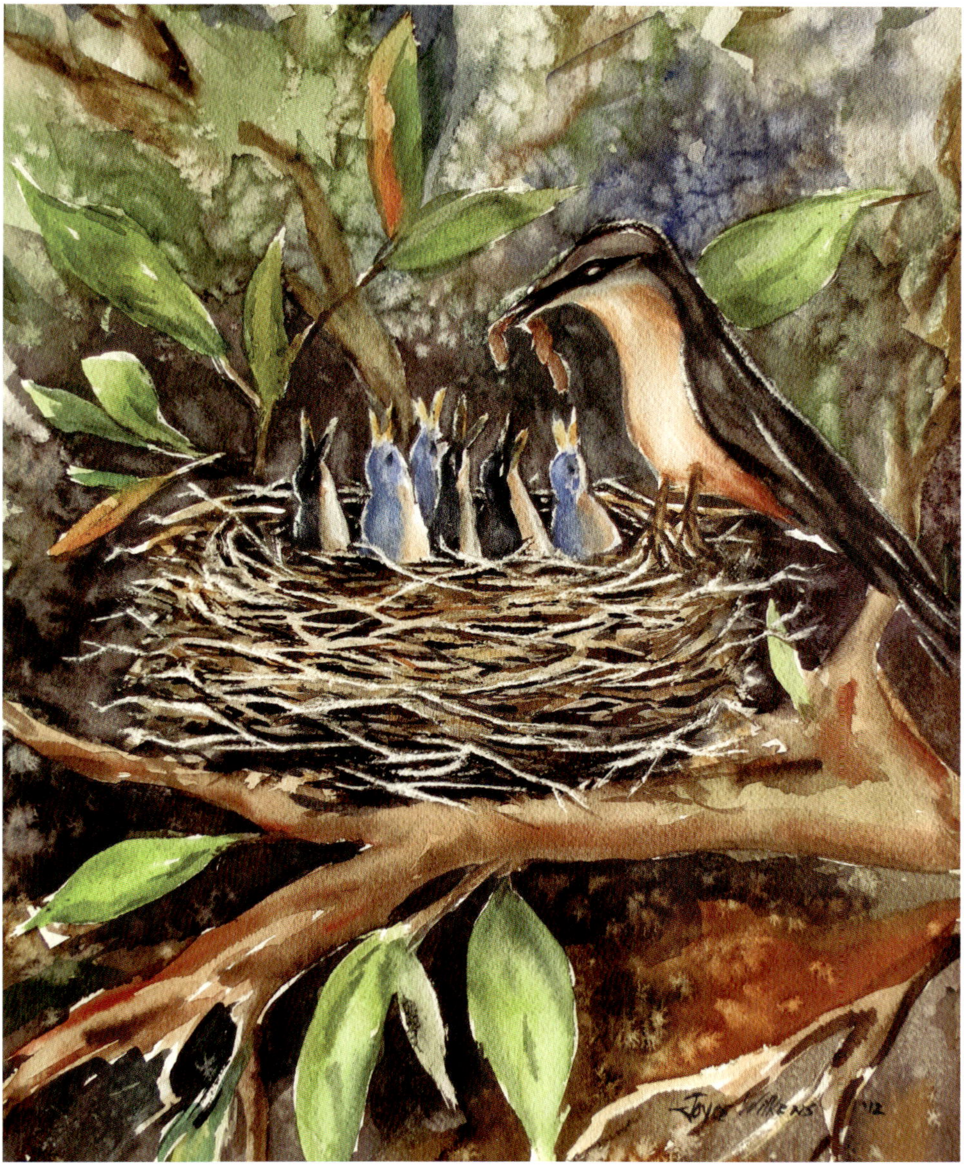

For love and care is giv'n to all,
Mixed in their colored hue.
And Springtime smiles upon this clutch
To bring it life anew.

Joyce Wilkens

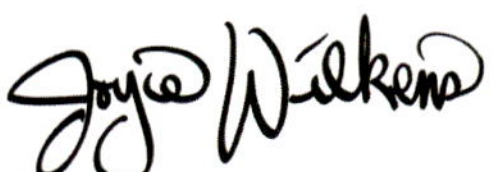

Trees

We think that there will always be
Many ways to see us trees.
Flashing our diversity.
Unique, comic artistry.

Cranky limbs so frequently.
Faces, curves, geometry,
In the core some symmetry.
Drawing comments thoughtfully.
Visual Thinking Strategy.

Oil, 3D cut canvases, branch slices, handmade frame.

Limericks by Nature

A limerick need not be unclean,
Off-colored, distasteful or mean.
But it should be fun
Or your work is not done,
So keep writing. It's best, it would seem.

And sometimes a limerick's political.
Quite often it can be satirical.
But written the most
Are the ones that can boast
Of lines humorous, wise, or nonsensical.

The first line of limerick will rhyme
With the second and fifth lines just fine.
The fourth and the third
Will each rhyme their last word
And complete the small poem in short time.

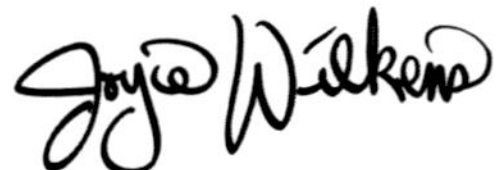

There's nothing like green grass so fair
For napping in fresh, open air.
But soon tiny ants
Find their way up my pants.
Oh, to linger, I really don't dare!

Oil

The leaves of the great maple trees
Do more than just sway in the breeze.
When nature does call
And there's nothing at all,
You'll be glad for the large maple leaves!

Oil

Peaceful Valley Tree Tunnel

Through my tunnel do you race?
The bus commute begins.
Or swiftly does your bike transport you
Through the leaves and limbs?

Maybe you're just wandering
To sense this valley's peace.
Then let the breezy branches bathe you
And your worries cease.

Possibly, on break from work,
You count your healthy steps
Into this green tree tunnel with its
Curvature and depth.

Hope you love this tunnel that
I've sculpted just for you,
And feel this artful arbor hug you
As you travel through.

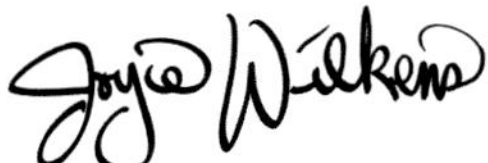

Wildlife Display

Stealthily, I tiptoe through
The woods that hug the creek.
I'm listening for some nature sounds
And dare not sing or speak.

Icy water tumbles down
And makes a chuckling sound
As sticks and logs will ride it 'til
They snag and run aground.

Rustling pines are muted as
The breeze now slips away.
My eyes are keenly searching for
A wildlife display.

(cont.)

Two Mouth Creek, Priest Lake, ID Oil

Then so unexpectedly,
My steps he must have heard,
He flies, then halts upon a branch,
A tiny hummingbird!

Frozen still in half a step,
My foot is in mid-air.
He looks me over— tilts his head.
Sweet moments then we share.

Thoughtfully I wonder why
He spends this time with me?
So am I now considered friend—
Or curiosity?

Friend, I think. He hunkers down
Upon the slender limb,
And doesn't seem to mind at all
That I've been watching him.

Seconds become minutes as
He locks me in his stare.
I finally plant my weary foot
That's lingered in mid-air.

(cont.)

Oil

Just as I am thinking that
These moments I'll embrace,
The tiny bird zooms off his perch
And drills right for my face!

Aaaaa . . . ch! My screams are muffled by
The creek that cares not why
I'm frantic to escape his wrath
And shelter valued eye.

(cont.)

Oil

Indian Creek, Priest Lake, ID

Crashing through the tangled woods,
I finally reach my car.
My screams then turn to laughter as
I ponder how birds are.

Wildlife encounters sure
Can take one by surprise!
And fierceness is not measured by
The loudness or the size.

Joyce Wilkens

Watercolor

I See You. Can You Love Me?

My voice is unique, spanning an entire octave in two notes. I belt out a hilarious song echoing through the hills. A smile hints at your delight. "Hee Haw." People think I'm inflexible. I suppose my stubbornness surfaces at times—OK, maybe more than a few times, but old age mellows me.

My disproportionate jawbone doesn't bother me.
The ancients used it in battle. And my short, stocky legs
wield a powerful kick if needed. I can easily carry your
heavy load. A "beast of burden" is my nickname.
Sometimes folks call me burro or ass. I like donkey, even
though that name also refers to the back end of a truck.

Do you know my history? My ancestors dutifully carried
many children, mothers, and grandmothers over the border
to find new homes. On a road once, my relative was confronted
by a flaming sword. That donkey stopped and spoke in a
human voice, thus saving his master who was unaware.

And an honored donkey carried one great man who
changed the world. I know what love is.
I see you. Can you love me?
Could you rub my nose and neck? It comforts me.
Come visit at the gate often. I'll wait for you.
Oh, and would you bring a carrot please?

Love,
A donkey

Oil

Ah, the painters' liberties.
With some simple strokes they tease.
Something odd is going on.
Two things here just don't belong.

Sounds of the Night

Where comes that sound? Yes, now I know.
His voice is soft and lofty though.
He does not sense I hear his call,
While listening from my bed below.

Who, who will keep me company?
He questions from the yonder tree,
And echoes through the darkest woods
To creatures only he can see.

(cont.)

Then silence lingers in the air.
So doesn't any creature care
To answer his most lonely plea
And travel to his treetop there?

Oh, neither squirrel nor mouse nor mole
Would ever think to leave its hole
And chance becoming fine cuisine.
The jaunt would surely take its toll.

But there! So faintly in the still,
Who, who responds from distant hill?
Ah ha! Companion. Perfect match.
Each other's needs they can fulfill.

Or did your shoes jump off the path
And take some joyous leaps and bounds?
Or bushwhack through uncertainty—
Some shifting sands and guarded grounds?

May I hear your story, please?
Tell me where your shoes have been.
Once I hear where you have walked,
I will understand you then.

Watercolor Palette

Deep inside the painter's palette,
Washed with greens and gold,
Are wild grasses, gilded beads
And stories to be told.

Leather boots and rocks and prairie.
Wire to enclose.
Or drops of blood. Then petals, too,
Of trampled, royal rose.

Violet purples form the mountains.
Fur of caribou.
The shadows hide the darks of past,
While heavens hail in blue.

Many ancient books will whisper
Pasts of yellowed age.
This palette rarely offers white—
Instead, uncolored page.

Run with the Wind

Run with the wind, my native child.
Meet Creator in the wild
Saguaro, sage and camas field.
Your spirit, body, soul be healed.

Run with the wind on pueblo ground.
Canyon echoes vaguely sound
Like muffled conversations past,
While stories etched remain amassed.

Lost. A tiny turquoise bead,
From your moccasin been freed.
Once woven with agave thread,
Now rests on earth—its journey read.

Run with the wind by river dome.
Sapling aspens craft the home
Which harbors dozing beaver babes,
Protected from coyote raids.

Run with the wind, my native daughter.
When you thirst for quenching water,
Sip from streams across your land.
But drink then from Creator's hand.

Life in Color

Love your life in color.
    Humanity in pale, brown, pink and the darkest of umber.
Love yellow for warmth, but heed it for caution.
    Its boundaries are edged with pot holes.
Love green, bursting fresh beginnings.
    Beware, though. Unhealthy want for what others have
    Will stain with a discontented shade.
Love blue. The world thirsts for it.
    Feathers and fins fly and dive through it.
    The universe is nurtured.
Love red. Passion's palette.
    The red rose of *I love you.* Speak it often.
    The crimson ground of life lost for others.
    Stand for purpose and remember sacrifice.
Love orange for zest and zeal—
    Artfully, masterfully ending the day.
Love royal purple. A worthy power
    From which to seek strength, refuge, rescue.
Love gray for it shapes the soul
    To experience other colors more brilliantly.
And black. Intensely defining.
    But find faith, choosing to live above
    the darkness of despair.
Love white. Blank pages when needed to rewrite
    the end of your story. White out past mistakes.
    Live happy. Love life in color.

The Reunion

They pose here to commemorate
A happy childhood history date.
There's fabric boy in painted plaid
And dotted clown so aptly clad.

And then, of course, a teddy bear.
In younger circles he'll be there.
From Roosevelt he got his name,
Which quickly brought him national fame.

Watercolor

Excitedly, she scoops them up,
The feathered, shiny eyes,
And ponders then what she will do
With her most treasured prize.

The day holds such adventures and
Some homemade bread and pie.
Then sadly, all too soon it's time
To thank and say goodbye.

Now back at home she heads to bed,
Her dreams to find their way.
The girl has one more thing to do
Before she ends the day.

Next morning when her mom and aunt
Come up to waken her,
They crack up as they tiptoe in.
The sight prompts quite a stir!

For there a princess soundly sleeps,
Most regal, it was said,
With peacock feathers standing up
Taped all around her bed!

I think I am a princess still,
No matter young or old.
His loving arms protect my soul
Until His hands I hold.

The Bread of Life

The Wild West Family

The happy, wild west family here
Will never spit and chew.
They'll try to smooth and keep the peace,
But dish out teasin', too.

They're law-abidin' citizens.
Respectful residents.
Their family roots are found across
The world's great continents.

The tallest poke can preach the Word,
And sings some guitar blues.
His red-head gal takes photographs
And writes creative news.

The ranch hand gently pulls your teeth
When, oh, they give an ache.
His dark-haired honey councils folks
And loves to cook 'n bake.

One cowboy helps the businessmen
And fiddles lots o' tunes.
His red-head sweetheart kindly works
To patch up bullet wounds.

And then there's Pa who always pays
A call when you get sick.
The light-haired Ma can brew some tea
And whittle a walkin' stick.

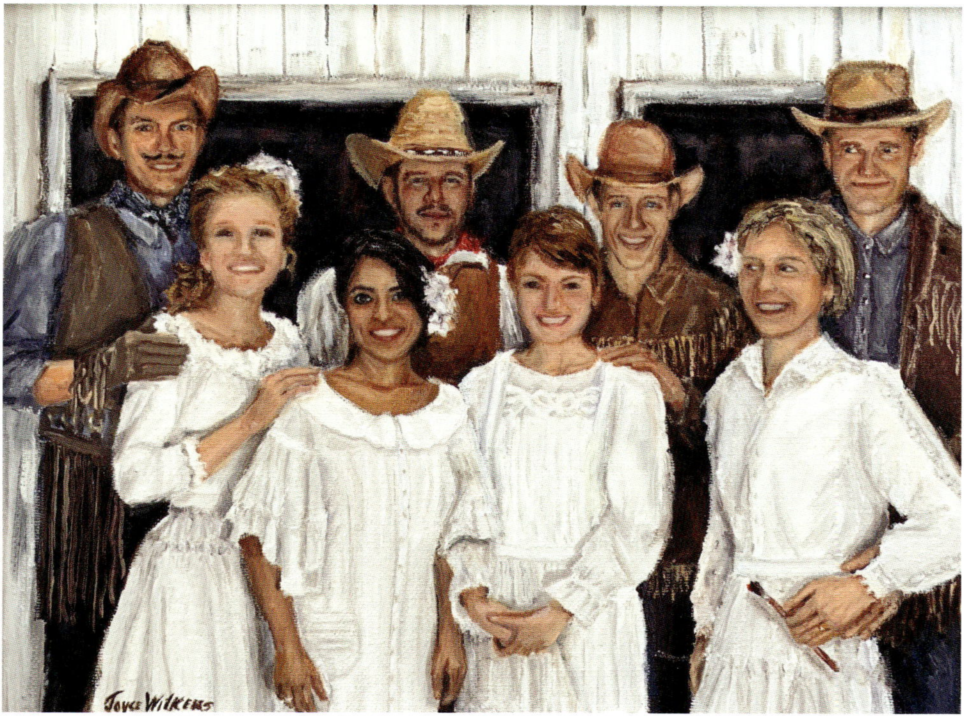

Oil

The family ties that strongly bind
Will hold when storms begin.
A higher power will ride beside
When they need rescuin'.

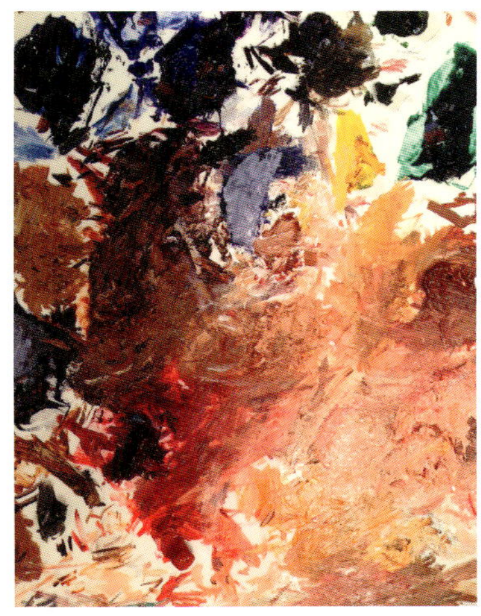

Or from the past, symbolic fleece,
Pulled from the saddle bag,
Might jog their memory to recall
The guidance that they've had.

And when the trail is closin' in,
Horizons they can't see,
Their faith will surely take 'em on
Into eternity.

Joyce Wilkens

Paint palette

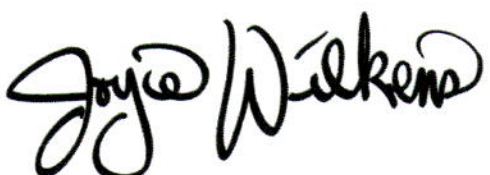

Retirement Together

When couples claim retirement in that momentous year,
Some questions ‘bout this time of life you just might like to hear.
Now that both have leisure time to fill their days with fun,
Consideration should be given to how things will get done.

Like who will do the laundry when it piles plenty high?
Or who will stock the pantry to replenish the supply?
Sometimes there are other tasks which call for specialty,
But many can be shared alike to foster harmony.

Oh, many of such questions are now swirling in my head.
Like who will clean the floors and sinks, and who will make the bed?
Breakfast served at crack of dawn? Or might it be a brunch?
And if they both are flexible, then who will make the lunch?

As health concerns take precedence regarding what they eat,
They might opt vegetarian, no sugar, leanest meat.
Some will grocery shop together, sharing tender smiles,
But others argue ’bout each purchase up and down the aisles!

Now, what about the travel plans, the bills and banking, too?
The weeding, mowing, sweeping—yes, an awful lot to do.
Vacuuming is just a must before guests come to call.
So will that job be jointly shared, or one do none at all?

Then think about some hired help. Now that could be a hit,
Though keeping bodies active still, of course, will keep them fit.
Tightening their money belts, the partners might agree,
To set up cash allowances to curb a spending spree.

So will one rise up with the sun—the other sleeping in?
And might one later on decide another job begin?
Volunteering twice a week. Perhaps it's just enough.
Or maybe use some leisure time to clear out years of stuff!

There also are some questions that a partner might just see
As hindering their freedom and their self autonomy.
Questions asked too frequently, then answered with a grin—
"Just don't ask where I'm going, and don't ask me where I've been!"

And one may want to travel far, explore and have a look.
Another might be quite content to see it in a book.
How to make together-time? Important thought, indeed.
Or how much individual time might fill a partner's need?

Yes, questions of retirement might need some clarity.
It seems the times require lots of flexibility.
Listen first. Some good advice. Consider feelings, too,
Then implement solutions that will work for both of you.

Life's well-worn luggage still holds joy, some pain and maybe tears,
But pack in lots of extra laughter in your Golden Years.
You can make a difference still, though technically "retired".
To make the world a better place—for that we say, "You're hired!"

Joyce Wilkens

Spiced Oldness

Our eyesight may have clouded now.
Sometimes our legs give way.
We grab an arm or walking stick
When balance takes a sway.

And often we can't clearly hear
Important things you say.
We may not even recollect
Your visit yesterday.

We sometimes lose our spectacles
And think they've been misplaced.
We search and search and finally find
Them planted on our face!

Oil

You might just think that underneath
These crumbling, old façades,
Reside our dampened spirits that
Are cranky, sad or odd.

But not the case! Ahead we see
A brighter future still,
And surely hope that mankind will
Find peace and love fulfilled.

We also like to sprinkle life
With just a touch of flair.
Oh, don't be fooled. We've still got spunk
Despite our graying hair!

Joyce Wilkens

The Ponytail

I jumped in the car with my daughter, one day,
And her two-year-old daughter in tow.
Her mom handed me a quite small rubber band.
She said, “Ponytail, quick! But no bow!”

Despite my attempts at a ponytail fast
Like her momma so expertly does,
My grand-treasure protested strongly against,
For she wanted her hair like it was.

I pulled my own bangs up on top of my head
And applied a quite large rubber band.
Just maybe she’d see that a ponytail’s cool,
And then quiet her wild, flailing hand.

It worked! She agreed! And we talked and we laughed
’Til we reached the appointment on time.
We signed at the desk. Took our seats with the rest
Of the folks seeing Doctor Divine.

For ten or so minutes, I noticed receptionists
Smiling and glancing our way . . . Ahhh.
They must be admiring my sweet little grand,
I most proudly concluded that day.

Or maybe they grinned—the resemblance they saw.
Generations of girls there we sat.
But then my sweet daughter leaned in to inquire,
"Mom, you know your hair still looks like that?"

Aghast, I pulled out of my pocket a phone
And I snapped a quick selfie to note!
That day I could not claim the title *Grandma,*
For I looked like a crazy *Grand-goat!*

Joyce Wilkens

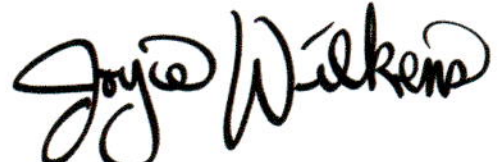

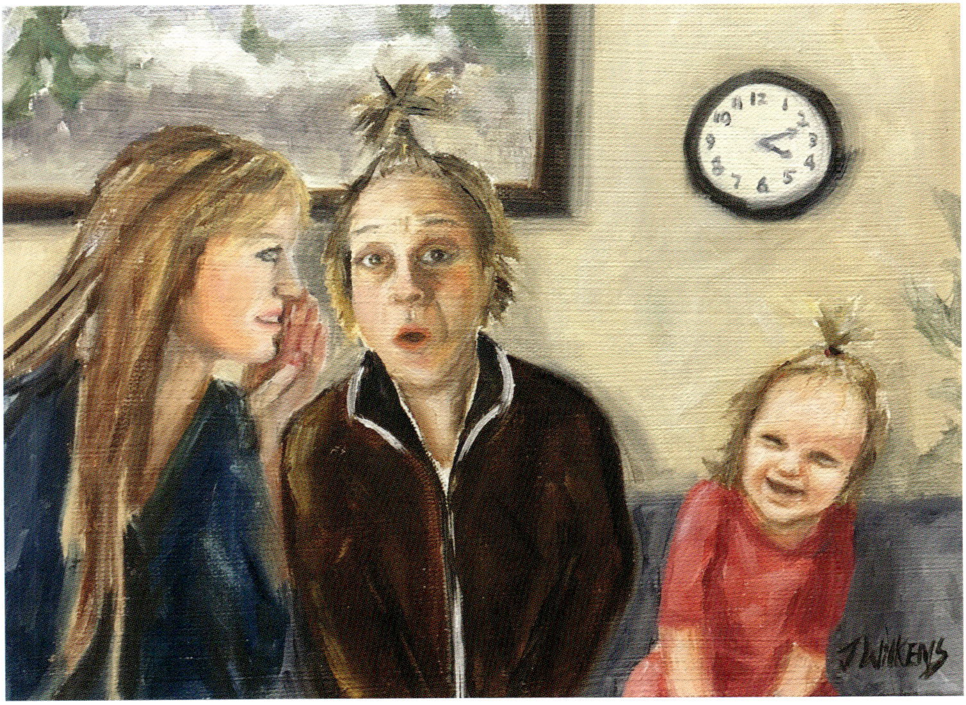

Oil

Oil

Raggedy's Run

Go! Seven and a half miles.
Careful. Swelling crowd.
Hear. Hoot and holler.
Band. Playing loud.

Pace. Watch the curb.
Downhill. Check your chins.
Pause. Tie a shoe.
Ponder. Tortoise wins?

Sky. Dizzy blue.
Tunes. Step some jigs.
Doom. See a vulture.
Crowds. High-five the kids.

Station. From the youngest.
Water. Cups and such.
Gulp. Drench the head.
Yell. "Thanks so much!"

Sprint. "Doing well!"
Strangers. "Photo please?"
Hot. Adjust the wig.
Relief. Cooling breeze.

Medics. On the ground.
Runner. Lying there.
Whisper. "Save the man."
Linger. Say a prayer.

Sweat. Round the bend.
Hose. Nozzle spray.
Mile. Marker seven.
Wave. Kids at play.

Speaker. "Raggedy Ann!"
End. Finish bold.
Smile. Look refreshed.
Consider. I'm too old?

Lines. Take a shirt.
Smile. Interview.
Search. Friends and family.
Pack. Andy, too.

Savor. All those years.
Rest. Quarter of century fun.
Retired! Thanks for memories!
Raggedy. Ann is done.

Princess of Americas

Princess of Americas,
As you wander west,
Foundations of the forest
Provide a place to rest.

Waters flow with peace,
Life and sustenance.
Your bravery and compassion
Portrayed with elegance.

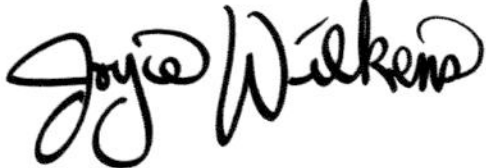

Oil

Oil

Queenly Monarch

Queenly Monarch,
Take your flight.
In the day a wanderer.
Resting in the night.

Friending Milk Weed
In the bay.
Colors—chemicals do caution.
Birds may stay away.

Flutter—passing
Splendid sites.
Sipping from the radiant flowers.
Winging windy heights.

Beaches beckon.
Warming sand.
Rocks and waters, trees and sky.
You will claim your land.

The Jimson

Ah! See the splendor bursting from the baking desert plain.
But toxic is the Jimson Weed. From eating, must abstain.
Still luring smitten artists quick to grab a loaded brush
And capture blooms awakening in dawn's low whispered hush.

The wind whips wild and sweeps the whites into a frenzied gale.
Each blossom shakes its rippled leaves and flaunts a curly tail.
For centuries you landscaped 'round some sweet adobe homes.
Your beauty will be brought to mind where'er an artist roams.

Oil

For ice-cream was heavily falling
On homes, every steeple and awning.
It froze up each street,
This vanilla cold treat,
With more chocolate and strawberry following.

It filled up the giant red wagon
And set the pavilion roof saggin'.
"Let's call Seed and Pet!"
Cried the town. "They might let
Us just borrow their great Bearded Dragon!"

His hot, muggy breath just might melt
All the ice-cream in town, it was felt.
The store said, "Okay!
He can blow it away,
This phenomenon nature has dealt."

His service he then did deliver.
He blew all the ice-cream downriver.
The pigeons and ducks
Drank from straws and big cups.
Ice-cream flowed to the town's Bowl and Pitcher.

It traveled five miles and then nine,
Soaking roots of the trees down the line.
It's true, I will tell,
Ice-cream flavors you'll smell,
If you sniff the warm bark of the Pine.

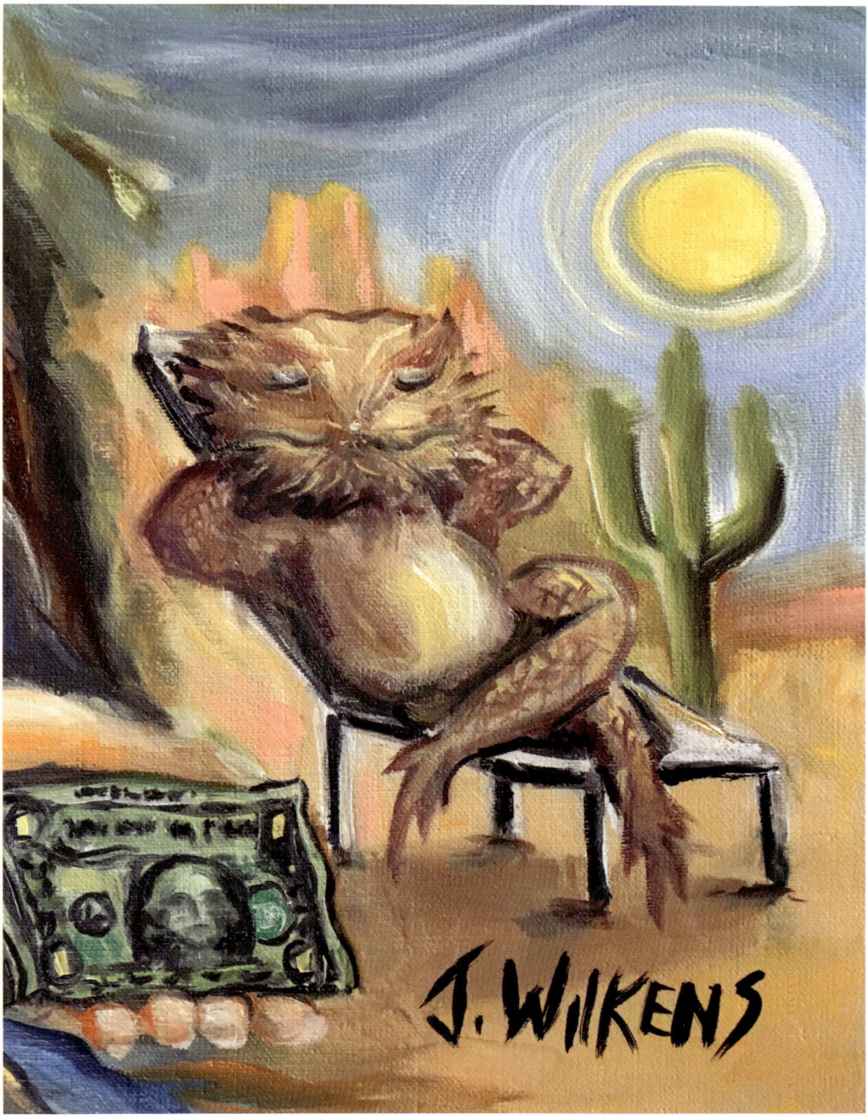

All cheered for the Dragon, "Hooray!
To him a great debt we will pay!"
So the town paid his price.
Now he lives in a nice
Arid climate in freedom today.

Joyce Wilkens

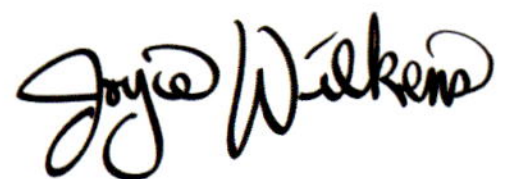

TRAVEL

Amalfi Coast, Italy Oil

Narrow, winding
roads that snatch
your breath away.

White
boats
hugging
bleached
cliffs.

Fuchsia pink
flowers and
saline breeze.

Turquoise
waters and
roadside
stands
laden with
yellow
lemons.
Small
cups of
tart sorbet
and tiny
tasting
spoons.

Venice, Italy Watercolor

Leisure, lapping water.
Venetian family life hanging out to dry.
Cracking, crumbling plaster clinging to medieval bricks.

Hole in the Wall, South Africa Watercolor

Hole in the Wall

Far in the reaches of South Africa,
There's a hole in the wall which elicits such awe.
Blue aqua waves push their way through to land,
And a wet, newborn goat runs and romps in the sand.
Wild Coast they call it. The breeze beckons all
To the vast Indian Ocean and hole in the wall.

Tunisia, Africa Oil

Camel Ride

Searing desert winds are breathing
'Cross Tunisia's plain.
For many days the blistering scape
Has begged for quenching rain.

Sky blue turbans hug their heads.
Shields from sand and sun.
They feel the soul of freedom as
Their camels start to run.

Now the cool oasis calls.
Calm the arid blast.
The bonded friends take pause just here
To make the memory last.

Oil

Camel Kiss

I ponder the need to be kissed,
For it certainly must not be missed.
"Don't do it!" they say.
"Step away! Run away!"
But the naysayers shall be dismissed.

For what is so wrong with a camel?
He's sweet and a hard-working mammal.
A bystander quips,
"He's got whiskery lips!
With bad breath and some brown-stained enamel!"

Too late. He moves in. Now I feel camel hair.
Plants a kiss on my cheek, sweetly lingering there.
Then laughter breaks out.
"Sanitizer!" I shout.
Yet—I smile at this moment so rare.

Joyce Wilkens

(A limerick poem)

Mexico, Oh Mexico

Mexico, oh Mexico, my heritage I know—
Spanish, Native Indian flow through from head to toe.

Mexico, oh Mexico, I tip my hat to thee,
For guacamole smothered chips and trumpet reverie.

Oil

“You must sit down! Do not get up
When seat belt light is on!”
Patiently, I watch the light
And wait until it’s gone.

Now as her destination nears
She slowly drops her feet.
Landing soon, she’ll join the flock.
Some others there she’ll greet.

I hope to board the bird again.
The bird with silver wings.
Longing for the sky view and
Adventures that she brings.

The bird with silver wings.

Joyce Wilkens

Hawaiian Aloha

Warm and wispy trade winds blow
And call across **Hawaii**.
Mixing blue and azure hues,
They swirl up in the **lani**.

Hawaii, Lani (sky).

Sculpting, twisting, bending all
The limbs of mighty **Koa**.
Wrapping me in welcome arms
And whispers of **aloha**.

Koa (Hawaiian tree), **Aloha** (hello, goodbye, love).

Restless clouds will fill their folds
And toss their showers of **ua**
On the birds, banana leaves
And vibrant, fragrant **pua**.

Ua (rain), **Pua** (flowers/flower).

Smiling, little **keiki** cling
To momma's **mu'u mu'u**,
While she sings and keeps the beat
With skillful hands on **ipu**.

Keiki (child/children), **Mu'u mu'u** (Hawaiian dress), **Ipu** (gourd drum).

Silent in royal waters swim,
O'opu grand of all.
Humuhumunukunuku-
Apua'a.

O'opu (fish), **Humuhumunukunukuapua'a** (Hawaii's state fish).

How I love the regal fish,
The turtle, graceful **hula**,
And the golden pineapple,
That sweet and luscious **hua**.

Hula (Hawaiian dance), **Hua** (fruit).

Ukuleles, drums and song
Resound from banquet **luau**.
Guests are welcomed with a **lei**
And feast on **ono kaukau**.

Luau (feast or party), **Lei** (string of flowers worn around the neck), **Ono** (delicious), **Kaukau** (food).

People of the land embrace
Integrity and **pono**.
Keiki, merchants, fisherman,
To wrangler **paniolo**.

Keiki (children), **Pono** (honor), **Paniolo** (cowboy).

Waters vast move in and out.
It swells, the great **moana**.
Crashing waves upon the reef,
While kissing swaying **pama**.

Moana (ocean), **Pama** (palm trees).

So I'll save these memories deep,
Oh, place of sun and sand.

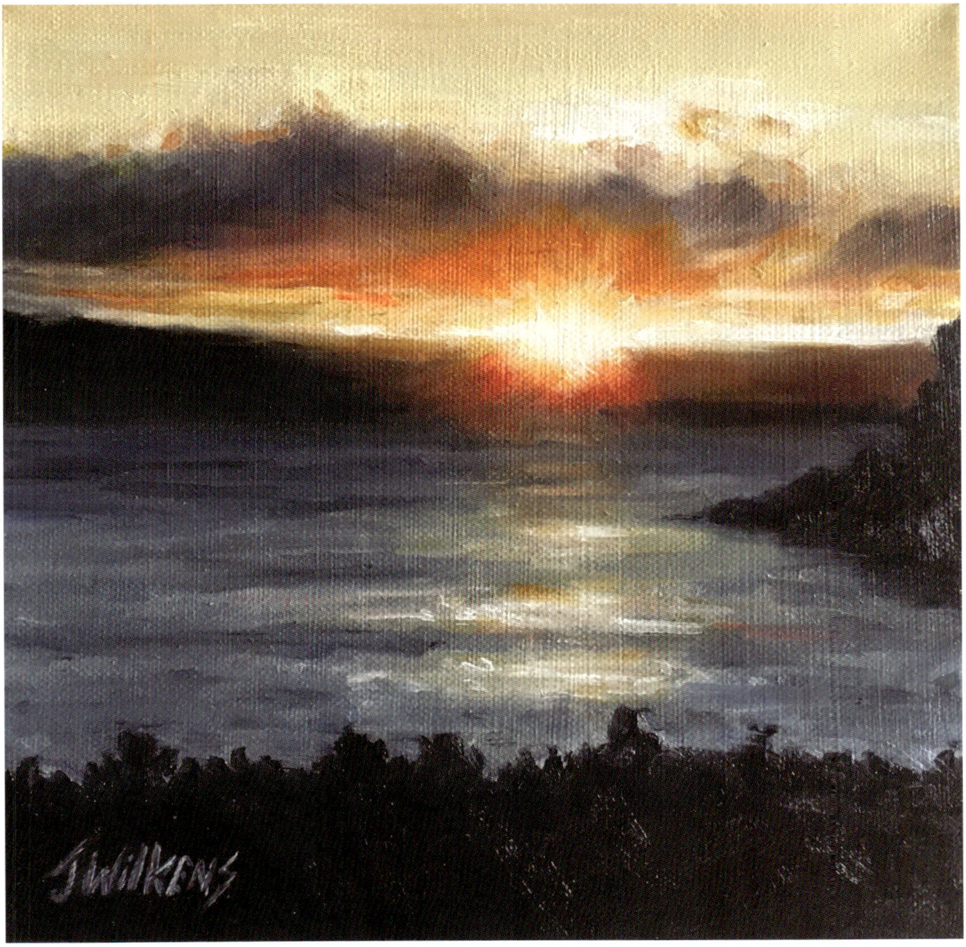

Footprints wash away, and yet,
My heart stays in your land.

LANDSCAPES

Paintbrush, Paddle, Boat, Berry, Rock and Dock

Fire, Fir, Sand, Smoke, Shore and S'more

Watercolor

The Painter's Moon

The moon mysteriously lulls the land
With captivating calm.
So silently it lingers low
At distance 'fore the dawn.
The rounded rocks reflect its light
By weathered, worn-out tree.
Alluring accent, oh, the moon,
A painter's prize indeed.

Varied Landscape

A photo is cut into three parts.
The first two parts are replaced with paintings using different styles of brushing.
The third part remains a photo.

Painting

Painting

Photo

Light of the World

Paint a vivid forest into my soul
And the generous light into my countenance.
Whisper the woodland flowers through my mind
And send a soothing sky into my rest.

The Caution Flag

"Do you need a flag of red?"
I ask my husband dear,
As I take note the length of wood
Extending from the rear.

"I don't think so," he replies.
He always knows what's best
When loading boards in pick-up trucks
And tractors and the rest.

I will ask this question, still,
O'er many a married year.
The answer's usually just the same
And spoken sweet and clear.

Sometimes, though, he says to me
A phrase that goes like so—
"If you can find a splash of red,
I'll add it 'fore we go."

Rags found in our pick-up truck
Are white or brown—not red,
And I'll not lend my fuchsia scarf
That's tied around my head.

"Not to worry. Rest your mind.
We'll add some white instead.
Let's take the slower route to home,"
Is what my husband said.

Later on I'm thinking that
I'll plan preemptively
For all those longer, lumber loads
With truck delivery.

Then I hit the local thrift
Of used, recycled stuff,
And shop with mischief in my soul
Until I've searched enough.

Found! I buy the splash of red
And proudly take it home.
(I cannot wait to tell you, now,
The ending of this poem.)

Forward several years—I get
A picture on my phone.
For there I see my man, so bold,
Has rigged a caution zone.

In his truck he's found my "flag."
It's perfect for his load.
I'm laughing that he's spreading joy
To others on the road.

Here's exactly what he did,
My spunky husband dear.
Onto his load he draped the "flag"—
An XL red brassiere!

Seeing comments like *Nice boards!*
Distracting! Oh, too fun!
Just maybe he will be inspired
To make another run!

Sure, we'll spice the landscape up
And not be too serene.
With grace and care and love we'll sculpt.
Such laughter in between!

Joyce Wilkens

Oil

Landscape Collaboration

They agree to collaborate.
An artist of fiber. An artist of paint.
Each must create
Using the medium of the other.
Stretch. Experiment. Explore.
Repeats. Repaint.
Dabble. Dots.
Mold. Mix.
Stone. Sticks.
Walk the land—the sand.
Imagination sifts or swells.
Fibers sing or sway.
Paint ripples or roars.
Landscape in collaboration.

Helen Parsons, Joyce Wilkens

Fiber and Paint

Landscape View

Do you usually view a landscape
With a casual glance,
Or will you stop to join the Aspens'
Frenzied, skyward dance?

Are the boulders mountain goats or
Hungry, brown-black bears?
Just maybe stacked-up river stones are
Ancient native stairs.

Do you search the landscape for that
Rare and radiant flower,
Or peek beneath a mushroom's ceiling?
Tiny fungus tower.

Landscapes hold a stunning cache of
Small and summit views.
I wish to do in-depth exploring.
Slow my hiking shoes.

With my love, we spy and wander
At a pondering pace.
Oh, look! Some small reflective landscapes
Framed upon his face!

Oil

BOATS

Oil

Love's Embrace

He pulls her close—this wedding day,
Pondering the vows they'll share.
Affection deep wells in his eyes.
The sun rays sweep her golden hair.

She's captivated by his soul.
Deeply feeling now the bond.
So savoring their fond embrace
And tender moments on the pond.

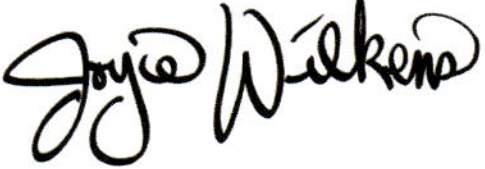

Watercolor

The Fisherman

Stubble chin and crooked smile.
Haven't bathed for quite awhile.
The fisherman.

Lacking sleep and home-cooked meals.
Blistered hands and tired heels.
The fisherman.

Rising waves and blowing storm.
Haul in nets before they're torn.
The fisherman.

Solid rigging holds the mast.
Finally get some sleep at last.
The fisherman.

There's a boat. Ahoy now mate.
Who's that there with hook and bait?
The fisherWOMAN!

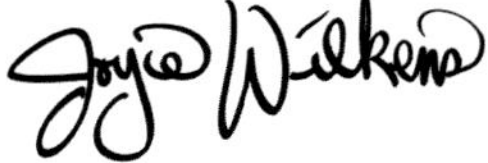

Charcoal

"Thank you, patrons, for graciously and generously supporting the arts!"

Joyce works from her home on the Palouse in Spokane, Washington. Her passion for creative story-telling, nature, beauty in expression and faith prompted her work as poet/artist/photographer. She loves every minute of it!

Mission work has called her to Selawik/Alaska, Mexico, Madagascar, Zambia and Zimbabwe. Joyce's art and books have journeyed to Saudi Arabia, Petra/Jordan, Israel, Thailand, Havasupai Canyon/AZ, to a US president, Egypt, Turkey and anywhere her shoes take her.

Her work as an art/history docent and actor for the Spokane Museum of Arts and Culture provided valuable education and experiences. In addition to **Poetry Pie,** she is author of coffee table book **Teacup Art,** as well as award-winning book **Walking Sticks.**

Joyce loves sharing the arts with the community, writers conferences, senior centers, classrooms, rotary/garden clubs, and church groups. Her photography, art and poetry can be found in homes, shows, publications, online and heard on radio. You can contact her or purchase books through her website.

JoyceWilkens.com